the Ranchería, Ute, and Southern Paiute peoples

Bertha P. Dutton is a distinguished anthropologist and expert on the archaeology and ethnology of Southwestern and Meso-American Indians. Among her many publications are *Sun Father's Way, The Pueblo Indian World* (with E. L. Hewett), *Happy People: The Huichol Indians,* and numerous journal articles and reviews.

Her work in the field has included research projects and excavations throughout the Southwest and expeditions to Peru, Bolivia, Ecuador, Panama, Guatemala, and Mexico, as well as attendance at conferences in South America, Europe, and the Orient.

The New Mexico Press Women presented to Dr. Dutton in 1971 the coveted Zía award for outstanding publications, and in 1974 she was appointed New Mexico representative to the National Park Service's Southwest Regional advisory committee by Secretary of the Interior Rogers C. B. Morton. She is a Research Associate of the Museum of New Mexico in Santa Fe; for a decade she served as Director of the Museum of Navaho Ceremonial Art, Inc., in that city.

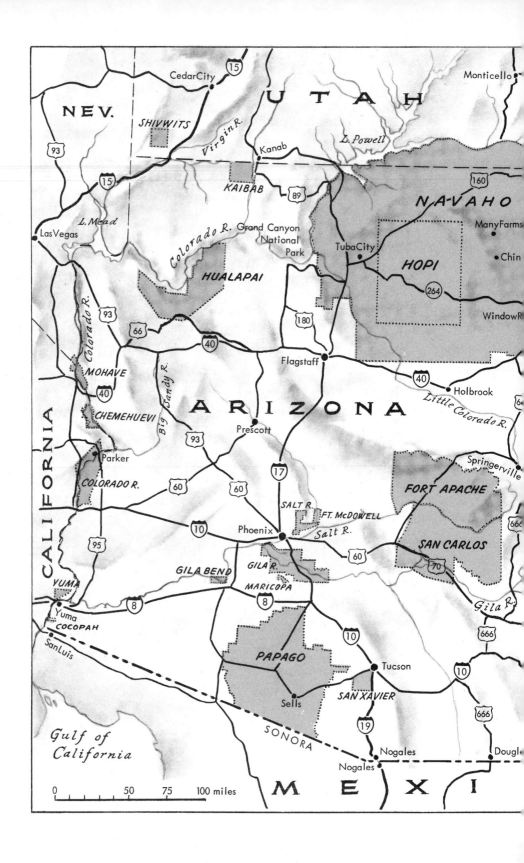

MAJOR INDIAN RESERVATIONS OF THE SOUTHWEST

This book and its two companion volumes, *The Pueblos* and *Navahos and Apaches: The Athabascan Peoples*, were originally published in one hardcover edition as *Indians of the American Southwest* (Prentice-Hall, 1975).

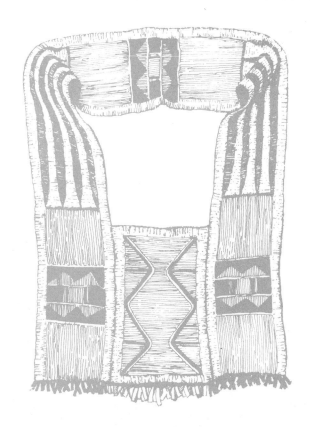

the Rancheria, Ute, and Southern Paiute peoples

Bertha P. Dutton

PRENTICE-HALL, INC. A SPECTRUM BOOK   ENGLEWOOD CLIFFS, NEW JERSEY

Library of Congress Cataloging in Publication Data

DUTTON, BERTHA PAULINE (date)
    The Rancheria, Ute, and southern Paiute peoples.

    (A Spectrum Book)
    Contains chapters 4-6 and a "Calendar of annual
Indian events" reprinted from the author's Indians of
The American Southwest.
    Bibliography: p.
    1. Indians of North America—Southwest, New.
2. Ute Indians. 3. Paiute Indians. 4. Piman Indians.
I. Title.
E78.S7D792 1976   301.45'19'7079   76-14988
ISBN 0-13-752923-0 pbk.

Cover photography: A Navaho sandpainting (Photo by Michael Herion)

Drawings: page 1—Ute beaded bandolier (Denver Art Museum: Cat. No. BU-66; *page 15*—Chemehuevi polychrome basket (California University Museum: NA8804); *page 23*—Detail of a Pima basket (Collection Sarah D'Harnoncourt, New York)

Printed in the United States of America.

10 9 8 7 6 5 4 3 2 1

Prentice-Hall International, Inc., *London*

Prentice-Hall of Australia Pty, Ltd., *Sydney*

Prentice-Hall of Canada, Ltd., *Toronto*

Prentice-Hall of India Private, Limited, *New Delhi*

Prentice-Hall of Japan, Inc., *Tokyo*

Prentice-Hall of Southeast Asia Pte., Ltd., *Singapore*

.... CONTENTS

This book
is respectfully dedicated
to
THE PEOPLE
. . . the original inhabitants
who revered this land
and its creatures
and strived to save and protect them

.........PREFACE

The objective is to make this book generally readable for students, teachers, and travelers who desire knowledge, understanding, and authoritative information regarding the Southwestern Indians; it is for those who wish to know the basic features of Indian life, but who do not, perhaps, have the time or specialized training to read extensively of these various peoples.

"The changing Indian" is much more than an often heard phrase these days. The *changing Indian* is a fact, an almost incomprehensible fact. And changes are occurring at such a rapid pace that whatever one writes may well be out of date before the words are printed. Thus it can be said that this publication is already outdated in certain respects. However, the decade census of 1970 afforded a pivotal point, and the statements made regarding the Indian groups of the Southwest are comparable as of that time.

Throughout this work obvious changes are mentioned, and some of the more covert ones are noted. Although these may vary in kind and extent with the different Indian peoples, certain features in particular are undergoing alterations and transformations: education, living conditions locally and away from the home bases; labor opportunities, industries, economic exploitation, road works, soil treatments, dams and irrigation; health, welfare and social security; old ceremonies and new religions; and in some instances reappraisal of cultural values, appreciation of old mores, and intensification of self-esteem.

The writer has chosen diverse ways of presenting the information assembled; the material is too exhaustive for a book of this scope to be complete. Emphasis has been given to certain aspects of one culture, outstanding facets of another; some of the main features of specific organizations have been portrayed, and the complex and far-reaching traits of the Southwestern societies indicated.

No attempt is made to give equal attention to each and every cultural group. Rather, the design is to show that all of the aboriginal peoples fitted themselves to their particular environment and strove to live harmoniously with nature. To all, the land was sacred. An eminent place was given to the mountains and hills, to the water sources and streams; to the plant and animal life; to the sky above and the celestial bodies seen traversing it, and to the clouds that brought summer rains and winter snows. The individual and the group were linked unconsciously with their surroundings.

And thanks were rendered for the orderly progression of season after season and for the blessings received.

The very way of life itself gave rise to keen observations, philosophical thinking; myths, poetry, song, and drama, which treat of simple things or the majestic; grief and joy, lullabies and love, with diversity of melody and of text. Each of these merits studies by itself. Some of the poetic contributions of the Indians are included, and of non-Indians who have been inspired by them. Something of the philosophy, drama, and other manifestations of Southwestern Indian life will be found in the following pages.

Not infrequently, secondary sources are cited as well as original works. These may be available to readers who wish to pursue studies regarding the Indians; and many will refer to primary works not included with the references mentioned.

It is hoped that reading this book will aid in an appreciation of the first Americans and of their intelligent responses to the surroundings; of their developments and attainments; and then of their tenacious attempts to continue living according to their philosophy and judicious practices in the face of white colonization, conquest, and alternating procedures of the Europeans whose aggressiveness, missionizing and political ambitions, and material desires were so foreign to the Indian beliefs of proper conduct and rewards.

Simply recording brief facts of history and taking note of modern conditions—some of which evidence accretions and others diminutions—have made the consistency of pattern apparent and impressive: peoples came from Asia, slowly populated the Southwest (as well as all of the New World), adopted ways of life in keeping with the conditions at hand, and developed social organizations thus dictated, recognized the limits of their domain and the rights of others, and achieved their respective cultural patterns. Then came the outsiders.

Every conceivable means has been employed to overcome the indigenous peoples and their mores, to make them conform to the white man's way of life. Through four and a half centuries, these efforts have met with relatively little success. Indians may be made to dress like Anglos, eat their foods, dwell in their types of structures, adopt their means of transportation, follow their prescribed curriculums and business methods, undergo the missionizing endeavors of various sects, practice non-Indian forms of government, and the like, but no individual or no aggregate body whatsoever can make the Indian be different from what he *is*. He may change—if he sees fit—or he may mask his feelings and appear to accept the Anglo customs; but the circumstances which produced the people that came to be called American Indians and the centuries that afforded them time to develop a racial identity and distinctive social patterns made an immutable imprint.

Regardless of outside pressures the Indians have remained Indians, and they always will. It appears inevitable that their resolute spirit will bear fruit, now that their numbers are increasing; that their pride in the accomplishments of their people has been intensified; and that they are beginning to discern their existent capabilities and power, and their rights.

ACKNOWLEDGMENTS The preparation of this publication has extended over a number of years. Much of the research and writing was done during 1971. After that period no further research was pursued. However, as certain individuals undertook the reading of the manuscript several months transpired between its completion and submission to the press. Suggestions of the readers were incorporated: these include later information on occasion, and the addition of certain references and bibliographic items.

As this work took shape, I began to realize how much I owe to the mentors with whom I have been privileged to study, to many Indian friends who have guided my research and added to the knowledge and understanding of their cultures, to my anthropology associates and those in related professions, and to the institutions and foundations that have provided funds for travel and research opportunities and have printed my contributions.

I am most appreciative of the fact that several busy people have taken time to read this manuscript critically and offer advice for its betterment. Among these I give special thanks to C. Fayne Porter, teacher supervisor in language arts at the Institute of American Indian Arts in Santa Fe, who is also a well-recognized author of numerous published works. To teachers in the same school, I likewise give thanks: Michael H. Clark and Paul W. Masters. Colleagues in my profession who have been particularly helpful are Robert C. Euler, Grand Canyon National Park, Arizona; A. E. Dittert, Jr., professor of anthropology, Arizona State University, Tempe, Arizona; John Martin, associate professor of anthropology at the same institution; and Dorothy L. Keur, former professor of anthropology, Hunter College, New York. Although they have not read the manuscript, these colleagues have been very helpful:

Bernard L. Fontana, professor of ethnology, University of Arizona, Tucson; David M Brugge, Curator, Navajo Lands Group, National Park Service, Chaco Center, Albuquerque; and Robert W. Young, student and teacher of Navaho culture.

Within the Bureau of Indian Affairs and the National Park Service, many persons and divisions have supplied information by means of correspondence, telephone calls, printed matter and photographs. Those to whom I render special credits are: Charles R. Whitfield, agency land operations officer, Papago Indian Agency, Sells, Arizona; Kendall Cumming, superintendent, Pima Agency, Sacaton, Arizona; William S. King, superintendent, Salt River Agency, Scottsdale, Arizona; Stanley Lyman, superintendent, Uintah and Ouray Agency, Fort Duchesne, Utah; Espeedie G. Ruiz, superintendent, Ute Mountain Ute Agency, Towaoc, Colorado; José A. Zuñi, superintendent, Hopi Indian Agency, Keams Canyon, Arizona.*

Other persons to whom I am most grateful are Al Packard, whose wide knowledge of Indian arts and crafts has been drawn upon extensively; William Brandon, writer, who has supplied several pertinent articles which otherwise might have been overlooked; Lloyd New, director of the Institute of American Indian Arts, who has furnished information and publications; and Constance (Mrs. William A.) Darkey, Edith (Mrs. William D.) Powell, and Dr. Caroline B. Olin, who have given editorial aid.

For supplying source materials and miscellaneous data, I wish to thank the Navajo Census Office, the Northern and Southern Pueblos agencies respectively, the Jicarilla and Mescalero Apache agencies, the Hopi Tribe, the Zuñi Tribal Council, the Northern Pueblos Enterprises, and many other contributors.

To Fermor S. Church, I owe an especially great debt. Without him this publication would not have been undertaken and completed. His training in engineering (degree from Harvard University) and extensive knowledge of the greater Southwest, its peoples, and its problems—which results from years of teaching at Los Alamos, Santa Barbara, and Taos; from managing the Philmont Boy Scout Ranch; serving in high positions with electrical cooperatives for over two score years; and publishing scientific articles—complemented my learning and experience. Our discussions of matters about which I was writing and manner of presenting them added much to the significance of this undertaking. Some of the maps were prepared

---

*Location of individuals at time of supplying information.

by him: the majority are by Phyllis Hughes of the Museum of New Mexico staff.

As author of *Indians of the American Southwest*, I have drawn on many sources and have quoted material extensively. Permission to quote direct statements was sought, and outstanding cooperation received. Sincere appreciation is expressed to the following authors and publishers:

American Anthropologist, American Anthropological Association, Washington, D. C.
American Antiquity, Society for American Archaeology, Washington, D. C.
American Folklore Society, New York
Arizona Highways, Phoenix
The Arizona Republic, Phoenix
The Caxton Printers, Caldwell, Idaho
Columbia University Press, New York (through a daughter of William Whitman III, Mrs. Philip T. Cate, Santa Fe)
Diné Baa-Hane, Fort Defiance, Ariz.
Frontier Heritage Press, San Diego, Calif.
Indian Tribal Series, Phoenix
Institute of American Indian Arts, Santa Fe
Museum of the American Indian, Heye Foundation, New York
Museum of New Mexico, Santa Fe
Museum of Northern Arizona, Flagstaff
The New York Times
The Progressive, Madison, Wis.
Southwest Parks and Monuments Association, Globe, Ariz.
Southwest Printers, Yuma, Ariz.
Time: the weekly newsmagazine, New York
The University of Arizona (Dept. of Anthropology), Tucson
The University of Arizona (vice-president for business affairs and treasurer), Tucson
The University of Chicago Press, Chicago
The University of New Mexico Press, Albuquerque
University of Oklahoma Press, Norman
University of Washington Press, Seattle
Robert W. Young and *The Gallup Independent*, Gallup, New Mexico

Specific citations are given with the references and full data appear in the bibliography.

To those who contributed their photographic works I am deeply indebted, including the renowned Laura Gilpin, of widespread fame, and Elita Wilson, who has produced outstanding records of the Southwest and its Indian peoples. These, and most of the other contributors, gave their photographs gratis for use in this publication; in other instances museums and other agencies made their contributions without charge. The name of each photographer or source appears with the pictures.

Grateful appreciation is acknowledged to those who typed the final manuscript copy of this work from the rough drafts submitted:

Mary Jean (Mrs. Edward S.) Cook, Rebecca Brown, and Sharyn (Mrs. Kimball R.) Udall.

LINGUISTIC NOTES

In pronouncing Indian and Spanish words, *a* is soft as in "father," *e* as in "grey," *i* as in "machine," *o* as in "whole"; no silent vowels occur. The consonant *h* is silent; *ch* is sounded as in "church"; *j* is like *h* in "hay." In *ll*, the first *l* is lightly sounded and the second takes a *y* sound; thus *Jicarilla* is Heek-ah-REEL-yah.

As noted by a recognized linguist who has worked on Southwestern languages for many years, Professor George L. Trager, "It is customary to refer to a people by the same form for singular and plural (as 'the Hopi,' 'a Hopi,' etc.)."

As with the spelling of the term *Navaho,* some writers follow the Spanish use of "j," though the word is not Spanish, while the modern trend is to use the English "h."

Santa Fe, New Mexico   *Bertha P. Dutton*

the Ranchería, Ute, and
Southern Paiute peoples

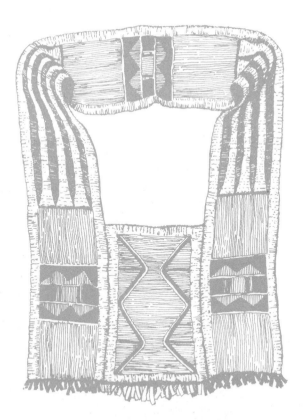

1 the Ute indians

In the state of Colorado, only the Ute Indians dwell today as organized groups. They are descendants of a people who once claimed about half of the area of the present state, two-thirds of Utah, and bits of northern New Mexico as their domain. They required a large geographical area to sustain themselves.

The Ute, who called themselves *Nünt'z* ("The People") had a food gathering-hunting economy; they wandered on foot, collecting plant foods and hunting game. Their struggle to survive took much of their energy and precluded extensive social development. All social behavior was defined or controlled by the family, often through an older member. Defensive war and the social bear dance were the only activities requiring the cooperation of a tribal unit larger than the family.

No overall political organization was ever achieved by the

Utes. They were divided into small bands, each with its own chief. Each band was an independent group. Among the larger bands whose names have come down through history were the *Uncompahgre*, or *Tabeguache*, whose central home was in the area around present day Gunnison and Montrose, Colorado; the White River and *Yampa* bands of northwestern Colorado; the *Mouache* who roamed along the front range of that state; the *Capote* who lived in the San Luis valley; and the *Weminuche* who occupied the San Juan basin of southwestern Colorado. The *Uintah* lived in eastern Utah.

After the Ute acquired horses from the Spanish immigrants, they were able to add greatly to their store of essentials. They became bison hunters and tipi dwellers. From 1630 to 1700, the seven bands consolidated into the Ute Confederation, and were able to transform from primary family units to warlike bands.

The Ute bands often fought with other Indians and sometimes among themselves. Generally they were friendly with the white men who invaded their mountain domain to trap, trade and prospect for minerals. But they were unprepared for the onslaught that was to follow. After the trappers, traders, and prospectors came the white miners and settlers who crept ever westward, until they occupied various areas on Colorado's eastern slope. In 1863, the federal government called a council of all the Ute bands; it was held in the San Luis valley. Fearing trouble between the whites and the Indians, the government wished to persuade the Utes to move out of these areas and to remain west of the Continental Divide. The government negotiators found it difficult to deal with the numerous chiefs. Finally, at government insistence, an Uncompahgre leader named *Ouray* (meaning "arrow") was designated as spokesman for all the bands. At first, Ouray and other Ute leaders declined to move away from the San Luis valley and the other areas which the government wished them to leave.

Reduction of Ute Holdings

Gradually, however, the Ute ceded most of their lands to the federal government to be used by white men for farming, ranching, mining, and the building of railroads and towns. Under a treaty made in 1868, the Utes promised to remain west of the Continental Divide. The treaty provided that virtually all of Colorado west of the Divide would be kept as a reservation for the Ute, with agencies established in the area of Gunnison and on the White river.

Before many years the treaty was broken by the whites. Gold and silver were discovered in the San Juan Mountains, and white miners invaded the Ute lands. A new treaty was negotiated in 1873, under which the Ute gave up the region in which minerals had been found.

The Mouache, Capote and Weminuche bands were consolidated on a strip of land along the Colorado-New Mexico border, fifteen miles wide and 140 miles long. There the Southern Ute reservation, with an agency near present day Ignacio, Colorado, was established in 1877. Almost all of those Ute people came to live in or near the Pine River valley. Principal leaders were Buckskin Charley of the Mouache, Severo of the Capote, and Ignacio of the Weminuche.

The Weminuche considered that region as their own, and from the beginning of this arrangement they resented the location of the Mouache and Capote among them. It was impossible for them to get along with the other two bands. Heeding the counsel of their chiefs, the Weminuche declined to farm, which was the intent of the government agents.

In 1879, the Yampa and White River bands, whose agency was on the White River near modern Meeker, Colorado, became restive. Goods and payments that had been promised by the government had not been delivered; and the insistence of the agent (N. C. Meeker) that the Ute become farmers even to the extent that he had their race track plowed up, led to eruption. Before the trouble ended, twelve white employees at the agency, including Meeker, had been killed. Troops under Major T. T. Thornburgh that were enroute to the agency were attacked and thirteen soldiers were killed before the Ute withdrew. We read of these happenings as the "Meeker massacre" and the "Thornburgh ambush."

Ouray, who became the most prominent of all Ute leaders, died near Ignacio while visiting the southern bands in 1880. As a result of the Meeker incident, pressure mounted among the whites to have all the Utes removed from Colorado. In 1881, the White River and Uncompahgre bands were exiled into eastern Utah to a reservation that previously had been established for the Uintah. By 1882, two-thirds of the Colorado Utes had been removed from the state.

As part of their scheme to make farmers and cattle raisers of the Ute by settling them on reservations, the federal government offered to allot each family land in the Pine River valley area. Those who accepted allotments got 160 acres of land, apiece. The Mouache and Capote bands, merged as the *Southern Ute Tribe*, remained on these lands. When Chief Severo died, Buckskin Charley became chief of both these bands. They gradually accepted the change from a nomadic life to an agricultural one. After the allotments were made to individual Indians in the Pine River valley, other reservation lands were returned to the public domain and were opened to homesteading by non-Indians. For many years the Southern Ute have lived as close neighbors of non-Indian farmers and ranchers (Spanish-Americans and Anglos).

The Weminuche, however, in 1895 chose to move to the arid, barren western end of the reservation, rather than accept allotted farm sites in the fertile river valleys to the east. With division of the original reservation, the Weminuche became today's *Ute Mountain Tribe*, with their own social organization and reservation. They have lived as stockmen, isolated to a great degree from non-Indians. On their western holdings, the "Ute Strip," the Weminuche eventually were furnished with an agency built at a point known as Navajo Springs, south of Sleeping Ute Mountain. About 1917 the agency was moved a few miles to the north, where a new community called *Towaoc* (meaning "all right" or "just fine") was established.

THE MODERN UTE PEOPLES

In securing up-to-date data for inclusion in this book, an effort was made by the author to obtain modern illustrative material. In very kind manner, I was told that: "The Ute Mountain Tribe is isolationist by nature and prefers to be left alone if at all possible. I questioned tribal officials as to whether they would permit publication of pictures of themselves, their homes or their ceremonials. They responded that they would prefer not."*

Although members of the Ute Mountain and Southern Ute groups speak the same Indian language, Shoshonean of the Uto-aztecan family, and have the same physical characteristics, they are two distinct entities. Each has its own tribal government and conducts its business independently of the other. Both groups were impoverished until recent years.

In 1950, however, the Confederated Ute Tribes (the two Colorado groups and the Northern Ute—those who had been exiled to eastern Utah and live on what is known today as the Uintah and Ouray reservation) won a $31 million judgment from the U.S. government as a result of claims for lands wrongfully taken in the

*I am indebted to the office of the Superintendent, Ute Mountain Agency, Towaoc, Colorado, for two mimeographed leaflets containing much of the information presented in this section: "The American Indians of Colorado" and "A brief history of the Colorado Utes." Other information was received in personal letters. (For general facts of the Utes of 1868, *see* Fowler and Fowler 1971:38-76, 110.)

mid-1800's. The Ute Mountain Tribe received about $6,266,000 in judgment funds after attorneys' fees were paid. The Southern Ute received around $5,500,000. And about the same time the land claims were awarded, natural gas was discovered on Southern Ute lands. Since then, oil and gas discoveries have enriched the Ute Mountain treasury also.

Following these events, both groups spent much time in studying ways in which their new wealth might best be spent for the benefit of their people. These studies resulted in rehabilitation programs which have brought about great improvements in living conditions. The people now live in modern homes. Health and sanitation standards have been raised. New roads have been built and old roads repaired. Tribal lands are being improved through good conservation practices. The children of the two groups have shared in the good fortune. They attend public schools, and scholarship programs of the tribes help young people who wish to attend colleges or vocational schools.

TRADITIONAL OBSERVANCES The old Indian way of life is fading on each of these reservations, but two annual events stemming from the ancient heritage of the Utes still are observed. These are the bear dance—the traditional welcome to spring—and the sun dance—a religious ritual that originated with the Plains Indians. The bear dances usually are held in April or May, and the sun dances in July or August. Since these are tribal festivals, rather than performances for tourists, the dates are not set far in advance. Each fall the Southern Ute hold a tribal fair to which visitors are welcome; and both they and the Ute Mountain Ute hold rodeos that are open to the public.

RECENT RE-ORGANIZATION Upon petition of the tribal councils concerned, and approval of the Department of the Interior, the Consolidated Ute Agency at Ignacio was split into the Ute Mountain Agency at Towaoc and the Southern Ute Agency at Ignacio. The change became effective on 29 December 1968. The agency staffs and other BIA personnel assist the tribal organizations in the fields of resources management (including soil and moisture conservation, land reclamation, irrigation, forest and range management, and realty problems), in community services (including welfare, education, and law and order), and in administration. The tribes receive certain assistance in health matters from the U.S. Public Health Service.

Joint objectives of the tribal organizations and the BIA are to give the Indian people greater economic security, to develop Indian resources to maximum productivity, and to help Indians take their place in American community life. It is said that both of these Ute tribes are making progress toward these objectives.

THE UTE MOUNTAIN UTE

The Ute Mountain reservation is located in the extreme southwest corner of Colorado, with a small extension into New Mexico. Most of the reservation lies in Montezuma county, Colorado, with the remainder in La Plata county, Colorado, and San Juan county, New Mexico. The location in general is high, deeply dissected tableland; the climate is semiarid to arid. A small number of Ute Mountain tribal members live in southeastern Utah on allotted trust land; although the allotments are not within the reservation itself they belong to the Ute and are considered as part of the reservation.

The reservation proper was established in 1895 by dividing the original Southern Ute Indian reservation. The established reservation is tribal trust land and has never been allotted to individual members. The total tribal holdings amount to 591,670 acres. These include tribal trust acreages of 448,030 in Colorado, 107,520 in New Mexico, and 2,328 in Utah, or 557,878 acres in all. Indian trust allotments add up to 9,459 acres in Utah, and 40 acres of government-owned trust, totaling 9,499. Tribal fee simple title lands total 24,293 acres. In addition, the tribe owns grazing permits on 132,695 acres of U.S. Forest Service and Bureau of Land Management holdings. The majority of the land is used for livestock grazing. A number of oil and gas leases are on tribal lands.

An elected tribal council with seven members has governed the Ute Mountain group since 1940, when a tribal constitution was adopted. The hereditary chief of the tribe, Jack House, although no longer an elected member of the council, has continued to have much influence in tribal affairs.

While the English language has come to be spoken, the common tongue is Ute. Much non-Indian attire is worn generally, but many of the women customarily wear shawls or blankets.

Reservation employment for wages consists of work for the tribal organization or the BIA. Self-employed activity is limited to stock raising with a very little farming. Revenue for the tribal organization comes from petroleum royalties and rentals and interest on tribal funds deposited with the U.S. Treasury.

The health of the population is good. Health care has been emphasized by the tribal government for a number of years, and is similar to health practices in general.

In the early 1950's, the average academic level of the Ute Mountain Ute was about fourth grade. Now the average is about sixth grade and is slowly rising. Younger children finish grade school, but the majority fail to complete high school. Concerted efforts by the tribal council, the tribal education committee, the BIA, and the public schools are helping, for more students reach the twelfth grade every year. Individuals are showing serious interest in vocational training, and several have taken advantage of programs offered by the BIA, OEO, and MDTA (Manpower Development and Training Act).

As of 1 August 1970, the tribal rolls of the Ute Mountain people listed 1,164 members; from this it has been estimated that the enrollment as of 1 January 1970 was 1,146 members. Of these, 778 live in Colorado, practically all in the community of Towaoc, the only reservation community. Some three hundred live in Utah. Descendants of small bands that always claimed the Blue Mountain region of Utah, and who refused to move to the Colorado reservation, reside on individual allotments of land at White Mesa in the vicinity of Blanding, Utah. The allotments were made in the 1920's and 1930's. There are some two hundred of these Blanding Ute —who are usually referred to as the Allen Canyon Ute.

Eighty-six Ute Mountain enrollees live on other reservations or off-reservation. Their closest ties are with the Southern Ute and the Northern Ute.

Inasmuch as other Indians, Spanish-Americans, and Anglos also reside on the Ute Mountain reservation the actual population was 1,187 as of July, 1970. Other Indians living in areas adjacent to the reservation bring total residency up to about 1,250 persons. Average family size is 4.7, and the average age in the tribe is sixteen years.

The council members of this reservation recognize that jobs are greatly needed. They are seeking industrialists to locate labor-demanding enterprises on the reservation. Presently, only few industries exist. Major resources include oil and gas from the San Juan basin, and "a spectacular extension of major archaeological ruins of the Mesa Verde type." The reservation adjoins the Mesa Verde National Park. Some timber is owned by the Ute Mountain Ute, but its economic value is uncertain. (Anonymous 1970b)

THE
SOUTHERN UTE

The Southern Ute Indian reservation also is in southwestern Colorado, occupying parts of La Plata and Archuleta counties. It has retained the fifteen-mile width of earlier times, but the length has been reduced to seventy-three miles. Within the boundaries of the reservation is some non-Indian land. The opening up of the reservation years ago to non-Indian homesteading resulted in an intermingling of Indian and non-Indian land holdings. In the 1930's the federal government returned to tribal ownership those acres contained in the Southern Ute reservation that had not been homesteaded. Of the present total of 818,000 acres within the exterior boundaries, some 307,000 acres are Indian land. Tribal trust land amounts to 299,443 acres; 4,967 acres are individually owned trust land.

The reservation lands vary from stream valleys to high mesas, with the most of the area at an elevation of between 6,000 and 7,000 feet. The climate is temperate and semiarid.

Since the reservation's establishment the people have relied on an agricultural economy based on cattle and sheep production, supplemented with some cash crops. Homes are built on irrigated farms in or near the Pine River valley. The land-base limitations and the general low economic level of agriculture in southwestern Colorado tend to prevent self-sustaining agriculture by a majority of the tribal members. For that reason, increasing tribal emphasis is being placed on development of employment-income producing enterprises in the fields of tourism and light manufacture.

In late 1971, a deluxe tourist center was opened at Ignacio. It includes

a 38-unit motel with meeting and banquet rooms, a pool, a lounge, a museum of Indian lore, an arts-and-crafts shop where guests may watch Indians at their native crafts, facilities for the display of motion pictures or slides, and a hall capable of accommodating four hundred.

In its auxiliary services, the tribe will supply fishing tackle and take its guests to the tribe's own Lake Capote for fishing. During big game season, guides will escort hunters on Southern Ute lands, and unexplored Indian ruins will be made accessible to guests.

Young members of the tribe were trained in tourist complex operations by restaurants, a motel, a hospital and the food service department of Fort Lewis College in Durango, 25 miles north of Ignacio. (Anonymous 1971b)

Aside from the dominant self-employed activities, wage employment is almost entirely of the service type, with the tribal organization and BIA being the principal employers.

In 1936 a tribal constitution was adopted, and since then the Southern Ute have been governed by an elected tribal council of six members. Their last chief, Antonio Buck, Senior, son of famed Chief Buckskin Charley, died in February, 1961. His position had been largely honorary, and the tribe has not chosen a new chief.

Revenue for the tribal organization is from petroleum royalties and timber sales and interest from tribal funds on deposit with the U.S. Treasury.

Enrolled membership of the Southern Ute is approximately 760, of whom about 600 are residents of the reservation; the remainder live in areas some distance from the reservation. Although Ute is the common language, most speak English. They dress as do their neighbors, for the most part, although a few of the women continue to wear shawls or blankets.

With the reorganization of agencies in 1968, the Southern Ute agency set up sixty-seven permanent positions, including twenty-nine people in school dormitory operations at Ignacio. This agency also provides some services to the Ute Mountain agency, such as plant maintenance when required. The latter agency has a staff of fifteen permanent employees.

THE NORTHERN UTE

The Northern Ute people live today on the Uintah and Ouray reservation, with agency headquarters at Fort Duchesne, west of Vernal, Utah, on U.S. Highway 40, approximately one hundred fifty miles east of Salt Lake City.

The reservation contains 1,008,192 acres of land situated in the Uintah basin of northeastern Utah. The elevation ranges from 4,655 to 9,200 feet above sea level, and the terrain varies from semidesert to forested mountains. In this environment, excellent hunting and fishing are provided.

On lands where the Uintah originally had been confined, the Uncompahgre and White River bands were moved by the federal government in 1881. Today about 1,200 full-blooded Ute of a total population of 1,600 reside on the reservation.

In 1952, the BIA closed the boarding school in Whiterocks. A few students attend off-reservation boarding schools. The six hundred school-age children are in public schools in the Uintah and Duchesne school districts.

Public Health facilities are located in Roosevelt, Utah, seven miles from the tribal headquarters. A clinic with full-time doctor, nurse, and dentist on duty is operated for walk-in patients. If patients are to be hospitalized, they enter a new County Hospital in the same building as the clinic.

The tribe has been very active in its economic development program. Its cattle enterprise is second to none in the state of Utah.* During the last two years, two hundred jobs have been opened on the reservation. The same period has shown a decline of about 23 per cent in the tribal welfare rate, and similar declines in the unemployment rate and arrest record.

The Ute Fabricating Company is a cabinet mill initially employing fifteen full-time employees, with an additional thirty men in training. A housing program under HUD was set to build one hundred fifty three-bedroom houses, eighty-six of which were to be completed by October, 1970.

The Ute people here have no intention of waiting for things or opportunities to come to them. Being developed in the center of the reservation is a multimillion dollar motel, restaurant, and recreational project called the "Bottle Hollow Complex." For this Bottle Hollow enterprise—so named because when federal troops were stationed at Fort Duchesne in the early 1900's, they hid their empty whiskey bottles in a gully near the site where the motel complex is being constructed—they have made sound and practical plans. Seventy members of the tribe were started in training for resort jobs, from desk clerk to lifeguard. Seventy more were to be trained as replacements.

The complex is in hexagonal form, employing a familiar symbol in Indian design. Fifty-two motel units form two large hexagons, one containing in its open center a six-sided swimming pool. Most of the furnishings of the motel—from beds to restaurant tables—are hexagonal. Included in the plans are an arts and crafts shop, service station, a combined restaurant-convention center, and a hexagonal plaza. Fishing, boating, and water skiing are made possible at a nearby reservoir.

Employees are given intensive courses in Ute history, English language skills, and the art of dealing with tourists. As these frequently cause problems for their Indian hosts, a former director of a hotel management school, and other instructors, were engaged to assist the Ute in learning how to keep even tempers. (Anonymous 1971d)

The Northern Ute participate in tribal dances throughout the

*The office of the Superintendent, Uintah and Ouray Agency, Fort Duchesne, supplied most of the information in this section.

year. Most common are the bear dances held in springtime. A traditional celebration is held on 4 July, with war dances and social dancing at Fort Duchesne. In the summer, the sun dance is held. The public is invited to all dances, but no pictures may be taken at a sun dance.

A few years ago, a group of mixed-bloods voted to sever relations with the Northern Ute Indians and with the federal government. These are known as the Affiliated Ute Citizens of Utah.

As with the Navaho and other Indians, the best way to learn more about the Ute people is to visit their homelands. Ignacio and Towaoc, the principal towns on the Colorado reservations, and the Roosevelt-Fort Duchesne area of the Utah Utes, are easily reached by good highways. The people will be found to be friendly and courteous if visitors are. Books on the Ute Indians are listed in the bibliography.

UTE BELIEFS AND CEREMONIES   The Ute bear dance, which is still performed by members of the Ute bands, has been mentioned. To gain information regarding this observance the reader is referred to an account given by a participant of the annual bear dance held in March, 1893, by the Southern Ute group. Mr. V. Z. Reed was an intimate friend of the then war chief and several other prominent members of the tribe, and was allowed to make a study of the dance. He could find no tradition antedating the dance itself on which the ceremonies were founded, but he believed the bear dance to be one of the oldest of all the Ute ceremonies. (Reed 1896:237) Indians came from far and near to participate in the dance. All except the smallest children danced.

Veneration of the bear, in one form or another, tinges many of the Ute ceremonies. The bear is regarded as the wisest of animals and the bravest of all except the mountain lion; he is thought to possess wonderful magic power. Feeling that the bears are fully aware of the relationship existing between themselves and the Ute, their ceremony of the bear dance assists in strengthening this friendship.

The bear dance was formerly held in March—when bears recovered from hibernation—under the direction of some one person. In olden times this was usually a medicine man or chief, who had a number of assistants. Then, too, preparations lasted for two or three months.

A site was selected for the dance, and an enclosure, or *a-vik-wok-et*, "cave of sticks," erected. It was circular, from one hundred to one hundred fifty feet in diameter, and represented a bear cave. Its one opening faced the south or southeast, toward the sun. The walls of timbers and pine boughs were built to a height of about seven feet; the enclosure was open to the sky.

Within this structure at one side, a location was selected for the stand of the musicians, and a concave hole was dug into the earth—simulating a cave. Over the hole a box or drum with an open bottom was arranged, and *moraches*, or "singing sticks," were placed with one end on the lap of a rhythmist and the other end against the box. Up and down the notched sticks, bones or pieces of timber are rubbed, making a rasping sound which the boxdrum amplifies. Reed described the sound as resembling muffled cymbals.

In his day, twenty or more musicians who had been specially drilled for the ceremonies sang and played their moraches. They were joined by others when old or familiar songs were sung; the singers were always men. The music, resounding in the little cave, is thought to be transformed to thunder, which arouses the sleeping bears in their mountain caves. The duration of the dance—four days and one night—was fixed by the time required by bears to recover from hibernation.

With the conclusion of the fourth day's feast, all ceremonies of the dance are over. The bears are felt to have fully regained use of their faculties, have found mates, have been provided with food, and it is felt that they will gratefully remember their Indian relatives and repay them by assisting in the practice of magic.

At the time of his participation in the bear dance, in 1893, Reed stated that in former times the dance was more exactingly observed than at that date. As one witnesses a bear dance of the present time, he may compare the observances with those of many decades ago. (*See* Emmitt 1954:34-40) The bear dances—traditional welcome to spring—continue on, although the time of celebrating has been altered somewhat, and the length of the ceremonies shortened so as to better meet the demands of modern life patterns.

The sun dance, a great summer ceremonial performed by Plains Indian groups, such as the Kiowa, Cheyenne, Sioux, Omaha, and others, was adopted by the Utes, adapted to their purposes, and continues to the present. The author had the privilege of attending the sun dance held near Ignacio, Colorado, July 1962, as a family member.

The fundamental object of the ceremony seems to be the over-coming of certain cosmic elements. All Indians performing it divide the ceremony into secret rites of one to four days' duration and a public performance. The secret rites include smoking, fasting, praying, and the preparation of objects that are to be used upon the altar or worn during the public performance.

On the last day of the secret rites a great lodge is built in the center of the camp circle, the selection of the site being the office of a special individual and attended with formal procedures. The ceremony of the sun dance abounds in symbolism, no rite being performed except in a prescribed manner. Of the sun dance in general, its ritual relates that once, in a period of famine an individual wandered forth with a female companion in behalf of his tribe, encountered a deity, fasted, learned the ceremony, returned to the tribe, caused the ceremony to be performed, and thus brought relief from famine through the appearance of the buffalo. The ceremony accordingly may be regarded as one of rebirth or reanimation.

It has been said that more than any other ceremony or occasion, the sun dance furnishes the Indians an opportunity for expressing emotion in rhythm, and for becoming more closely united.

Like the Navaho, the Ute people have taken over peyote ceremonialism.

SPEAK TO ME

O trees, say something.
One day you move back and forth,
Another day you are still.
How can I tell
What you are thinking, feeling?
Please speak to me.
Lovers carve names in you.
That must be painful.
I sit beneath your branches on sunny days,
When the wind blows and
Your leaves whisper and fly away,
Waiting for you to speak to me.
Are you angry at everybody?
Do you feel pain or delight?
Oh trees, please speak to me.

By Calvin O'John, Ute-Navaho

From: *The Writers' Reader,* 1962-1966, The Institute of American Indian Arts. Santa Fe, N.M.

SOUTHERN UTES AND COLORADO RIVER INDIANS

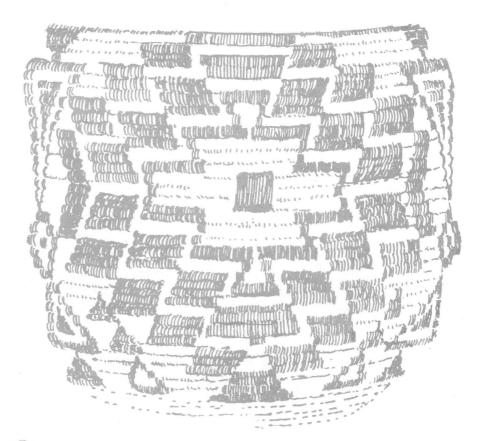

2 the Southern Paiute

Linguistically the Southern Paiute belong to a Numic-speaking group of the Shoshonean branch of the UTO-AZTECAN stock. It was said by J. W. Powell that the name Paiute properly belonged exclusively to the "Corn Creek tribe" [Pah-vants] of southwestern Utah, but that the term had been extended to include several other Shoshonean-speaking peoples. (Hodge 1910) In general "Southwestern Paiute" has been applied to Ute-Chemehuevi groups. Since we are writing of the Southwestern Indians of the Four Corners States, attention is given only to those Paiute peoples of northwestern Arizona and southwestern Utah, although others of Paiute classification live in southwestern Nevada and parts of southeastern California.

Archaeological investigations and linguistic evidence have shown that "these Numic speakers spread across the Great Basin into the northern portion of the Southwest some time shortly after A.D. 1000, replacing prehistoric Pueblo or Pueblo-like peoples who had earlier lived in the region. In extreme southern Nevada and southwestern Utah, archaeologists have excavated the distinctive ceramic remains of the Southern Paiute in direct association with those of the Pueblos made around A.D. 1150. The Paiute pottery was brown or reddish-brown, conical with pointed bottoms, and often decorated with rows of 'finger nail' incisions. This is easily distinguished from the highly decorated black-on-white, black-on-yellow, or polychrome pottery of the Pueblos." (Euler 1972a:2)

It is probable that Southern Paiute people learned to raise corn and certain other products from the Pueblo Indians, making it possible for them to initiate a semisedentary living pattern. Rude defensive features found at some of the mid-twelfth century pueblos suggest that strife may have arisen between the two groups, causing the Pueblos to leave the region and the Paiute to add to their holdings eastward. Primarily, the Paiute were wild plant gatherers and hunters of rabbits and mountain sheep—for which they used long bows and arrows and long nets. Their homes were probably temporary camps and, to some extent, along permanent streams where they could farm. Excavations have brought forth grinding implements with which seeds, piñones, corn, and meat were ground and pounded. These milling stones differ from those used by the Pueblos. Southern Paiute-Hopi relationships appear to have existed on a friendly basis from around A.D. 1300-1600; trade was a major factor in their contacts.

The Southern Paiute were little disturbed by the Spaniards, with whom they came in slight contact during the sixteenth and seventeenth centuries. Father Escalante, who traversed their territory in 1776, seems to have been the first European who attempted to describe them systematically. He went through southern Utah a few miles north of present day Cedar City, and met a seed-gathering party of Southern Paiute Indians. (Bolton 1950; Euler 1972a) Later he encountered the Kaibab group.

In the same year, Father Garcés visited southern Paiute people known as the Chemehuevi, who dwelt near the Mohave on the lower Colorado River. It has been noted that Garcés "made it clear that the Chemehuevi, in the 18th century anyway, did not distinguish themselves from the Southern Paiute in the Las Vegas, Nevada, area immediately to the north." (Euler 1972a:18)

After the U.S.A. annexed New Mexico and California, the Paiute domain was encroached upon steadily, and some of the

Indians were placed on reservations. The majority, however, remained scattered through their country. Friction between the Paiute and the whites was minor until the 1840's, when it increased greatly. (Euler 1966:44-74)

Recently, it is said, only about 1200 Southern Paiute still survive. A shabby settlement in Cedar City, Utah, bespeaks their current state, "too few to wield political power, too poor to pay for legal advice." The government cut them off from federal benefits in 1956, and it has been noted that:

Without birth certificates, Social Security numbers, or land deeds, they couldn't collect welfare or negotiate loans. For that matter, they didn't even know how to qualify for hunting and fishing licenses to seek food in the mountains and streams of their forefathers.

At the same time the federal government emancipated the Paiutes, it declared they were unable to manage their own affairs and directed [a bank] . . . to sell their reservations. (Anderson 1971)

The Indian Peaks band sold their 10,000-acre reservation for $40,000.

The few women here who made basketry—a craft already on slim grounds—encountered further calamity. Due to extensive use of pesticides by farmers or government agents who sprayed the vegetation, including the requisite materials for basket making, several of the basket makers became ill from drawing contaminated willow twigs through their teeth. As a result, they were forced to go as far as central Nevada to find DDT-free materials. To make the trip, the older women at least had to depend upon someone with a car to take them. This and other factors have resulted in the decline of basket production. (Fowler, C. 1971)

The Kaibab Paiute   Just north of the Grand Canyon in Arizona, bordering on Utah, the small Kaibab group is located. As late as 1869 this branch of the Southern Paiute had scarcely seen a white man. They were seminomadic, with a hunting and food-gathering economy. They did some fishing, so their food consisted of fish, jackrabbit and other small game, piñones, and seeds that were ground into flour for bread. Their dwellings were brush shelters erected upon poles planted in the ground, or upon an interlocking pole tripod conical in shape. Shelters were very temporary and frequently in summer none were used.

The geographical location kept these a poor, unorganized people, unable to resist the white man's settlements pushing into their domain and usurping their water. For years, they lingered in their original habitat near the new villages being founded by Mormons in northern Arizona and southern Utah. Cattle, sheep, and farming of the white man caused the destruction of their native foods, making life increasingly difficult. Gradually they attached themselves to the Mormon communities. As they were peaceable, of high moral character, and industrious, their willingness and efficiency made them necessary to the white farmers. Apparently the Paiute had little or no religious organization, and as a consequence the Mormon efforts toward conversion met with some success.

Mormons who settled in the 1860's at Moccasin Spring—the water of which the Paiute had used exclusively for centuries—forced the Kaibab group to move and become nomadic; they made their base in and near Kanab, Utah. Some time later, but prior to establishment of the Kaibab Reservation in 1907, Mormon church officials negotiated a deal with the squatters at Moccasin Spring, whereby one-third of the flow of the spring was granted to the Paiute and they were permitted to farm a small tract of land, watering it from the spring. (Euler 1972a:84, 87) Thus the Indians came to practice a little agriculture, with some irrigation. The BIA issued cattle to them at the time the reservation was established. A good herd was built up, but soon disseminated. Another herd, purchased in 1916, had become reasonably successful by 1930, but the depression that followed and the war of the 1940s lowered the Kaibab Paiute to a state of mere existence.

Foremost of the Paiute arts was basketmaking, including conical baskets for carrying burdens, parching trays for roasting seeds, water jars, hats, and semi-basketry cradles for babies. As elsewhere in the Southwest, basket making is passing from the scene. Pottery production was always minor. Formerly, extensive use was made of animal skins for clothing and, to some degree, shelters.

A social event—the round, or circle, dance—was held, and games were played.

In time, the Paiute reluctance to accept a changing way of life was overcome. Progress has come rapidly. Numbering 136 (in 1972), the Kaibab Paiute continue to live in small groups on their 120,413 acres of reservation land west of Fredonia, Arizona, on U.S. Highway 89. All commonly dress in western garb today.

The Kaibab Paiute operate under a tribal constitution adopted in 1951, with a council of members of either sex elected annually. The officers are: a chairman, vice chairman, secretary-treasurer, tribal judge, and chief of police. The council meets each month in

Fredonia. The chairman is the only salaried employee of the tribe.

Their tribal headquarters is at Moccasin, in the west-central part of the reservation.

Under provisions of the Indian Claims Act passed by Congress in 1946, the Kaibab and several other Southern Paiute groups filed suit against the government of the U.S.A., "claiming restitution payment for all their aboriginal lands that had been wrongfully taken from them by the Government or agents thereof." (Euler 1972a:92) The case was not decided until 1970. but the Indians won and a judgment was received. With a land claim settlement of slightly more than a million dollars, the Kaibab appear to be destined for better times. It has been said:

Today, some fourteen families, comprising sixty-two people, live in the small settlement of Kaibab, two miles from Moccasin Spring. The remaining seventy-four individuals live nearby. While a few still live in small, frame houses, ten other families reside in attractive and recently completed "self help" concrete block structures. The main roads are paved, thus easing transportation problems especially in the snowy winter months. A spacious tribal administrative building was officially dedicated on June 2nd, 1970, providing adequate offices and meeting facilities for the tribal council and other employees.

Reservation lands are not yet used to their full economic potential. Until recently, approximately 10,000 acres of grazing land were leased to non-Indian ranchers but the remainder was not in any type of production.

There are two private enclaves within the Kaibab Reservation boundaries. One of these, 400 acres, comprises the Mormon settlement of Moccasin. The other tract, of 40 acres, is the National Park Service facility of Pipe Springs National Monument, an early Mormon "fort" around a small spring.

The Kaibab Paiutes receive medical and dental care through contract services with physicians and dentists in nearby communities, a program financed by the U.S. Public Health Service. There is also a resident P.H.S. community health worker on the reservation.

Paiute children—and of the total population of 136, forty-four are under the age of 16—attend a one room public school in Moccasin. From the sixth grade through high school, however, they are bussed to Fredonia, twelve miles to the east. Approximately 10 Paiute children are not in high school and four others are attending college. (Euler 1972a:92-94)

Opportunities for producing individual income on the reservation are limited. A few Indians are employed by federal or state agencies. Other than for those, stock raising provides some income, and men for the most part derive wages from work on nearby ranches owned by white men.

Expecting the land claims funds to alleviate some unemployment, the Kaibab Tribal Council has allocated 15 per cent of the total claim payment to per capita distribution. "This amounts to slightly over $1,000 per individual. An additional 15% has been budgeted for a 'family plan.' These funds are distributed by the council to enable families to pay off past debts, obtain household furnishings, and other immediate family needs. Both of these budgeted items are being released to the Paiute at the present time. The remaining 70% of the land claim monies are being budgeted as follows: Education, 10%; Tribal Enterprises, 35 %; Community Development, 15%; and Administration, 10%. None of these funds has as yet been expended. (Euler 1972a:94)

The Shivwits Indian Reservation   In the very southwestern corner of Utah, on a desolate 27,000-acre reservation, a Paiute people called the Shivwits are located. They were only beginning to have contact with the whites by 1870. When their land was offered for sale some years ago through a Salt Lake City bank, no one who wanted to buy it could be found. (Anderson 1971)

Theirs is plateau land, through which the Santa Clara River flows. U.S. Highway 91 leads through the reservation from Saint George, Utah, to the Arizona and Nevada borders. Between 150 and 200 are on the census roll. They live in brokendown shacks.

THE CHEMEHUEVI INDIANS   Chemehuevi is the Yuman name for a group of Indians who were a part of the true Paiute, and were associated with them and the Ute in one linguistic subdivision of the Shoshonean tongue. (*See* Fowler and Fowler, 1971:5,7) They called themselves *Tántáwats*, meaning "southern men."

Anciently, they lived in the eastern half of the Mohave Desert, and it has been estimated that there were between 500 and 800 of them. They lived in small huts of Paiute type, usually low shelters covered with dirt and of temporary nature. Their means of subsistence was seasonal plant-gathering and hunting, with a few attempts at growing meager crops near springs. (Stewart 1967:14) They made excellent baskets. In 1776 no Chemehuevi lived on the Colorado River below Eldorado Canyon. Later, they settled on Cottonwood Island, about fifteen miles north of Davis Dam, in the Chemehuevi valley, and at other points on the Colorado River. Here they were under strong Mohave and Yuma influence (these are discussed in the following section).

It is reported that although the Chemehuevi continued to stress basketry, they began to imitate the Mohave in making a few pottery vessels, quite in the Mohave manner. The men started to wear their hair in Mohave fashion, rolling it into thin "ropes" that hung down the back. They took over the use of tule rafts and log rafts, and "the Yuman practice of ferrying goods and children across the river in large pots." The Chemehuevi had known the practices of interment and of cremation; they followed the Yumans in cremating bodies and possessions of the deceased in a special rite, and in a mourning ceremony wherein images of the dead were housed in a special structure. (*See* Drucker 1937)

Another source states that, "Once on the river the Chemehuevi seem to have become a more definite political entity, with a chief called the *towintem*, who had more authority or at least more influence than Chemehuevi leaders had previously possessed." Their religion took on Mohave characteristics; they began to sing song cycles which told of mythological events, in the Mohave manner. And "like his Mohave counterpart, the Chemehuevi shaman dreamed his power to cure." (Stewart 1967:16) The Chemeheuvi also adopted certain Mohave modes of making war.

On 2 February 1907, the Chemehuevi Indian Reservation was created by the Secretary of the Interior, and became the home of the Chemehuevi. It was located roughly halfway between Parker, Arizona, and Needles in San Bernardino county, California. Then, in 1940, the river bottom lands totaling about 7,776 acres were sold to Los Angeles Metropolitan Water District and deeded back to the U.S. government for control. The Chemehuevi were paid $108,342 for the land. Eleven allotments—the only ones ever made on the Chemehuevi reservation—were assigned within the river bottom area. They were all sold and the land is now under water. The balance of the reservation—approximately 28,000 acres—was not productive without expensive irrigation facilities.

With the construction of Parker Dam on the Colorado River, which was completed in 1938, virtually all of the arable acres came to be inundated by the water of Lake Havasu. Insofar as was known in 1970, only one Chemehuevi was living on the reservation. The others were moved to the Colorado River Indian Reservation,and became enrolled members of the Colorado River Indian Tribes. It is estimated that the membership includes 600 Chemehuevi.

The Chemehuevi observe no tribal or religious ceremonies. Recently it was found that only one old basket maker remained of the tribe.

AS ONCE, SO WERE WE

We are the native Americans;
This was our land from sea to sea.
Our thoughts were all thoughts,
As once, so were we.

But time seemed to change
When the white man came;
Came he, mighty in strength,
As once, so were we.

"Never mind," said my father,
"The world will go on."
And he chanted and prayed
and sang his death song:

The Earth is my Mother,
She will always be near.
The Sun, my Father,
I have nothing to fear.
The Moon is my Sister,
Standing with me at night.
The Stars are my Cousins
Who guide me in flight.
The Great Spirit is my God
Of life and of love.
We will soon be with Him
In His land up above.

By Raymond Hamilton, Mariposa-Paiute-Tuolumne

From: *The Writers' Reader*, Fall, 1966, The Institute of American Indian Arts, Santa Fe, N. M.

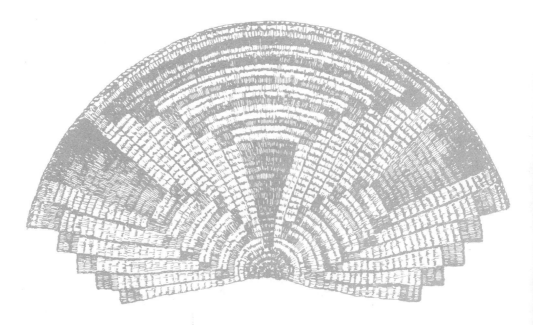

3 the Rancheria peoples

In contrast to the Pueblo peoples, the great majority of aboriginal dwellers of southern Arizona (and northwestern Mexico), although equally sedentary, did not live in compact, closely built settlements. Their houses might be scattered at some distance from each other, thus forming loose settlements here and there on the farmlands, or *rancherias*. A group occupying these locations might shift from one ranchería to another during the course of a year. They were all agriculturists, with farming their major activity. Among these peoples, as among the Pueblos, many similarities obtained. Especially in their economy were they alike; in community structure they were more disparate. Most of them spoke languages belonging to the UTO-AZTECAN stock, such as the Pimans and Cahitans. But, other than these, the Yumans belonged to another linguistic family, the HOKAN-SIOUAN. Their range was to the northwest of the other ranchería peoples.

THE COLORADO RIVER
.... INDIAN TRIBES

The Colorado River Indian Reservation was established by Act of Congress, and approved by the President on 3 March 1865. The boundaries were subsequently fixed and determined by Executive Orders dated 22 November 1873, 16 November 1876, and 22 November 1915.

The reservation lies in a valley along the lower course of the Colorado River. Although surrounded by mountains, the valley is definitely desert with an elevation of approximately 400 feet above sea level. Characteristic vegetation of the valley consists of cactus, mesquite, and *chaparral*, or dense thickets of thorny shrubs; arrowweed grows along the river. Average rainfall is about four inches per year. No snow falls in the valley, but the surrounding mountains are sometimes capped with light snow in the wintertime. The average humidity is generally 15 per cent, but at times it runs between 55 and 60 per cent. The mean temperature averages 71° F., ranging from an average minimum of 56° to an average maximum of 86°, the average extreme maximum temperature being 97°. In December and January the average low temperature is 39°, and in June, July and August, the average high temperature is 110-113°.

The first expenditure of federal funds for irrigation development in the U.S.A. was made for work on this reservation in 1867, with fifty thousand dollars being spent. All the work was done with shovels and baskets by about five hundred Indians. Because of faulty design and an unusually high water level in the river, the canal washed out as soon as the gates were opened. In 1874 another canal was completed; it too met with failure. Additional appropriations followed for canal construction, pumping facilities, engineering studies, and construction of Headgate Rock Dam, a diversion structure that was placed in operation on 4 July 1942.

In 1873 the first school on the reservation was opened.

During World War II, the War Relocation Authority built camps on the reservation and relocated approximately nineteen thousand Japanese there. These camps were closed and the Japanese removed in 1944. A year later, sixteen Hopi families were relocated on the Colorado River Indian Reservation. During subsequent years, one hundred and fourteen Navaho families and three Havasupai families were colonized on irrigated lands on the reservation. The program was ended in 1952.

The Colorado River Indian Reservation is approximately 264,250 acres in size, with 225,914 acres located in Yuma county, Arizona, and 38,366 acres situated in San Bernardino and Riverside counties, California. The reservation agency is headquarters for the Fort Yuma Subagency, Yuma, Arizona (located on the Fort Yuma Indian Reservation, California), and for the Indian reservations of Fort Mohave (Needles, California), Chemehuevi, and the Cocopah around the mouth of the Colorado River (Somerton, Arizona).

THE FORT MOHAVE RESERVATION

This reservation is situated along both sides of the Colorado River, being partly within Mohave County, Arizona; San Bernardino County, California; and Clark County, Nevada. The land generally extends from a point across the river from Needles to a point about fifteen miles north of that city. The part west of the river begins some five miles north of Needles and is divided into two areas—one in California and one in Nevada. The northerly part of the lands is an integral area, while the southerly part, east of the river, is a checkerboard area, the sections alternating. The terrain is desertlike with brushy first bench land and river wash areas as well as portions of the river channel.

Agency headquarters is in Parker, Arizona, and the Mohave tribal offices are in Needles. The Fort Mohave Reservation was established by Executive Order, 19 September 1880. Another order of 1 December 1910 enlarged the reservation, but one of 2 February 1911 revoked that order and added other lands to the reservation. Then an act of 8 July 1940 granted the right to take specific Mohave lands within the reservation that would be needed for construction of the Parker Dam and Reservoir, up to the 455-foot contour line. "At no time did they intend or authorize a taking for any other purpose. Nevertheless, when the trustee later issued an order designating the Mojave* lands needed for the authorized purpose, no mention was made of the 455-foot contour limitation. Instead, the specified lands were erroneously described by metes and bounds, thereby resulting in an unauthorized seizure of several thousands of acres of Mojave land." (*See* note on following page.)

Then, we are informed:

Very recently, the Indian Claims Commission declared that title still resides in

---

*See the Linguistic Notes on p. xxix.

the Fort Mojave Tribe in regard to the several thousand acres of land to which reference has been made.

There are two categories of Mojave land included in the several thousand acres thus seized without authority: (1) Indian lands occupied and fenced by the Fish and Wildlife Bureau of [the] Department [of the Interior] far exceeding the area flooded by Parker Dam and in no manner required for that purpose; (2) Lands which have been flooded for which no compensation was paid. (Fort Mojave Tribal Council 1970*)

The present reservation of 38,382 acres is owned in undivided shares by tribal members, and is held in trust for them by the federal government. A total of 511 people live on the reservation. That their claims to title have not had due recognition or protection from the federal government is observable through one injustice after another that the Indians have suffered for more than the past three decades.

In 1962, when a case arose between the Indians and the U.S.A., the U.S. Attorney, purportedly in behalf of the Indians, abandoned their cause and argued against them. Primary results were that the Indians lost possession of lands (which many think should be returned to them) and a legal barrier has been interposed, denying them redress in present claims—which have received no support, apparently, from the Justice Department. The Indians state that:

Seizure by the United States, trustee of Fort Mojave Indian Property, has transpired throughout the entire reach of the Colorado River as it traverses or borders upon the Fort Mojave Indian Reservation. That seizure stems in part from acquisitions by the Bureau of Reclamation in the name of the United States which have cut off entirely or gravely impeded the Mojaves' access to the Colorado River to which they are legally entitled. Loss of access is tantamount to imperiling for all time the full economic potential of the Mojave lands.

There are at least seven substantial areas in which the right to access of the Mojaves to the Colorado River has been seized in its entirety or gravely impeded, all as stated above. In all, there are approximately 12 miles of land lying on both sides of the Colorado River where the irreparable damage to the Indians as described above has taken place.*

The Secretary of the Interior, as the principal agent for the U.S.A. and trustee for the Indians, was beseeched to "take speedy and adequate steps fully to assert on behalf of the Mohave Indians their rights of access to the Colorado River which have been seized from them without authority." (Fort Mojave Tribal Council 1970*)

*Letter of 27 October 1970, as follow up of an urgent telegram sent about six weeks before to the Secretary of the Interior.

THE MOHAVE PEOPLE

The Mohave and Yuma peoples spoke a different language from that of the Chemehuevi, being of the Yuman linguistic group of the HOKAN-SIOUAN family. It is said that the Mohave called themselves *Tzi-na-ma-a* before they came to live along the Colorado River. "Mohave" is taken from a native word, *hamakave*, referring to Needles, and signifying "three mountains." (Swanton 1952:356) These people came to dwell on both sides of the stream, mostly on the east side, between Needles and the entrance to Black Canyon. Theirs was a ranchería type of life. Early Spanish explorers mentioned their villages. Oñate met them in 1604-1605, and Garcés found their settlements in 1775-1776. (Galvin 1967:v, 12ff.) No Spanish towns or missions were established in the Mohave territory. The Mohave were said to number 3,000 in 1680 and 1770.

The earliest Anglos to enter Mohaveland were fur trappers and fur traders. They came from 1826-1834, but their visits had slight effect on Mohave culture. It was the coming of others, after the midcentury, that caused uneasiness among the Indians. In an encounter with soldiers in 1859, many of the Mohave were killed. From 1900 on, they apparently decreased steadily, and their enrollment shifted from one Indian agency to another.

The Mohave of Old

In their initial state the Mohave subsisted by small scale farming, gathering of wild plant foods, trapping, and hunting and fishing. A hunter never ate what he killed. Floodwater irrigation was utilized in the production of corn, melons, pumpkins, and several wild herbs. When floods did not occur and crops failed, the people ate mesquite beans; they ate beaver, but would not eat turtles, snakes or lizards as did the Chemehuevi and other desert dwellers.

The Mohave had hereditary chiefs in the male line—men of honor and dignity—but their functions are said to have been obscure. Much more influential were the brave men, war leaders, and shamans. Their enemies were the Cocopah, Pima, Papago, and Maricopa. Friendly peoples were the Yuma, Chemehuevi, Yavapai, and western Apache.

Homes of the Mohave were built of logs and wood, with roofs thatched with arrowweed and covered with sand. They were usually about twenty by twenty-five feet in size, and the door was always to the south because of the frequent cold north winds of the desert.

The Mohave attire generally was similar to that of other lower Colorado River peoples, but had its own characteristics. Both men and women commonly wore loincloths, covering the upper body only in inclement weather; they went barefoot and bareheaded. A woman's dress was made in two parts—separate back and front aprons of willow bark strips hung from waist cords. The front piece fell to the knees; it was donned first, with its cord tied in back. The calf-length back apron which was thicker was tied in front; it lapped over at the hips but left the outside of the thighs somewhat bare. A short underapron was worn at all times beneath the front apron; it was made of fine willow bark.

The breechclout of the men was held in place by a belt, the ends forming a short flap in front and a longer one in back—to the knees or below. These were made of willow bark strips in a checkerboard weave. When an upper garment was worn—a privilege of only a few—it was of rabbitskin strips held together with cords, obtained by trade from the Walapai Indians, or a wool poncho bartered from the Navaho. Sandals were worn by men and women only when traveling. No leggings were worn, nor hats. Sometimes men tied downy feathers or quills to the crown hair of their heads.

These people were long famous for the artistic painting of their bodies. Some tattooing was also done, though it is rare now.

Crafts and Implements Pottery was made by the Mohave in at least three distinctive forms. A strong association was felt between their pottery and their agriculture. A harvest of food was not complete until bowls had been made for cooking and storing it. The men and women worked together. Clay had to be tempered with crushed sandstone, and the pottery vessels were built up by the coiling process; they were decorated with a yellow ochre pigment, which turned to a dull red upon being fired—by means of an open wood fire.

Mohave basketry was very poor, both in quality and in its paucity of types; none is made today. The only true basketry receptacle made was a flat tray, slightly oval in outline, some eighteen inches broad at the wider end, and two feet long. These were made of slender willow twigs twined at intervals with split willow twigs, and a rim was fashioned of a thick willow branch bound on with long split mesquite root strands. The trays were used for sifting chaff from ground mesquite pods or corn, or for cooling parched seeds. A netted structure supported by a framework of sticks served as a carrying frame. A headring used for carrying was made of willow bark; women used these to bear the forehead band of the carrying frame, or to support pottery or other burdens carried on the head, including the baby cradles when carried lying flat on the head. Otherwise cradles were held horizontally on the hip, never on the back.

When imported glass beads became available, the Mohave accepted them eagerly. To this day they do beautiful beadwork.

Gourds in a variety of shapes were used for carrying water and storing seeds. Globular gourds were made into rattles, with a wooden handle inserted in the stem end and fastened with gum of greasewood and arrowweed. Two parallel rows of tiny holes formed a decorative cross on the body of the rattle.

The Mohave used slim shinny sticks with moderate curve. Their bows were shaped like a shallow *D*, nearly straight for most of the length and tips curved toward the string. The bow staves were made of willow or screw bean (*tornillo*), or mesquite. Length of a bow depended upon the height of the man who carried it—the ideal length being from ground to the chin. Hunting bows were shorter than war bows, averaging three and a half to four feet. The Mohave had great interest in warfare; they were brave and had notable leaders, or war chiefs. Their fighting was primarily hand-to-hand, when they could charge upon their enemies with war-club and bare hands, or the bow and arrow. (Spier 1955)

Dream Life   In addition to their concrete day-to-day living, they set great importance upon their dream life; and even today they passively drift away without external inducement, such as drink, drugs, dancing or costume garments. From these dreams—which to the Mohave are regular visits with their ancestors—come their decisions and their principal motivations. Religious interest revolves around funeral ceremonies, in which they cremate their dead with rites and loud wailing; the meager supply of personal belongings is burned with the owner.

Changes in Attire   After a time, the basic agricultural products were expanded to include beans, cantaloupes, and wheat. With the improved economy, other changes took place. The older women wear long, full dresses of bright print, with scarves on their heads. When a death occurs in the family the women may cut their hair which, otherwise, is worn long and straight. The older men dress as most westerners, with denim pants, western shirts, boots, and large hats. The younger men and women and the children dress as do their white contemporaries.

The People and Their Ceremonies

The Mohave men are inclined to be tall, large-boned, and lean. The women are not so tall and are prone to be stout; they have good-natured faces. Skin color is of a noticeably yellow hue. The people are responsive, energetic, and smiling.

Most of the ancient Mohave ceremonies have become extinct. A bird dance has been preserved, and is colorfully performed by a small group, carefully costumed, at celebrations and public gatherings. Several times during the decade of the 1960's and into the 1970's, this group presented its dance at the Intertribal Indian Ceremonial in Gallup, New Mexico.

Altogether, the present cultural picture is in sharp contrast with that of the past. (*See* Brennan 1966)

Political and Economic Development

The Chemehuevi, the Mohave, and the Hopi and Navaho Indians enrolled at the Colorado River Agency, Parker, Arizona, and living harmoniously together on the Colorado River Reservation constitute the Colorado River Tribes. They number 1,620, of whom 1,120 live on the reservation. They accepted the Indian Reorganization Act, have a constitution, and hold elections on the first Saturday of December every second year. The adult members vote, using the secret ballot. Their council, which governs the reservation, is made up of nine male and female members; it meets the first Saturday of each month at 9:00 a.m., in Parker.

They have six active committees, each with its chairman. Tribal operations relate to tribal government, enrollment, and claims; the improvement of social, economic, and political status; and the assuming of greater responsibility in the management of their own affairs. Programs under way include Community Action, Community Development, Headstart, and NYC (Neighborhood Youth Corps). They have their own code of law and order, tribal police and tribal court.

A new tribal administrative office building and a library have been built about a mile south of the agency. Across from these is a recreation center with a large building where fairs, socials, carnivals, and other events are held; there, too, is a baseball field and bleachers, an outdoor basketball court, and an outdoor stage for shows and contests. North of Parker the Indians are in the recreation business in a big way; they operate the Bluewater marina, with *cabañas*, trailer park, restaurant, gift shop, a boat launching pad, and judges' stand for boat racing. The Indians are attractive, gracious, and efficient hosts and hostesses. They are exceptionally progressive and farsighted, and are making great progress in their program to become entirely self-sufficient.

The winters here are so mild that fishing, boating, and picnicking continue throughout the year. (*See* Brennan 1967) Several motorboat races are held during the spring, and a two-day rodeo in November. Hunting is good on the reservation (ducks, geese, quail and doves), as is fishing. Permits are issued for these sports.

It is the general mission of the Colorado River Agency to administer Indian affairs within its jurisdiction, in cooperation with the Indian people in planning, executing, and coordinating the BIA's extensive and varied programs. These cover education, welfare, law enforcement, soil and moisture conservation, range management, irrigation, extension, forest management, road construction and maintenance, realty, credit, plant management, development of local self-government and tribal undertakings, industrial development, employment assistance and vocational training.

Land and Water The most important single program, probably, has to do with the maintenance of subjugated lands and the development of more such land. In this, the operation of an extensive irrigation system, carrying water diverted from the Colorado River on the Arizona side, and hydrographic investigation, surveying, construction of facilities, drainage and seeding activities are said to be of paramount importance. The Indians have shown marked ability to take advantage of the latest advances in farming, such as use of modern equipment, methods, fertilizers, and insecticides. Several packing sheds operate in Parker during various harvesting seasons.

The U.S. Supreme Court has ruled that the Indians have "perfected water rights from the Colorado River" and permission to grant long-term leases to non-Indians: twenty-five years for residential land, ninety-nine years for recreational and commercial land. (Brennan 1967:18) Fifty thousand acres are now farmed by the Indians for themselves or lessees, and 107,000 acres are guaranteed a first-class irrigation system for the future. Market crops of alfalfa, barley, cantaloupes, carrots, cotton, corn silage double-cropped with maize, lettuce, and small grains are reported in truly fabulous yields and all the year round. Ten thousand sheep are wintered and cattle are fattened for market in feed lots. All prospects point to brilliant success, according to the most modern standards . . . if the Mohave can withstand the machinations and rapacity of the white men and the governmental agencies which they control.

Recently, like so many other of the Indian peoples, the Mohave and the Chemehuevi have developed a new awareness of their former cultural products. In 1970, upon learning of a collection of Mohave beadwork and pottery and Chemehuevi baskets which had been assembled by a pioneer storekeeper in Parker, Arizona, and was being auctioned off in Phoenix to settle an estate, members of the two Indian groups mortgaged their best land to raise fifty thousand dollars with which to purchase part of their heritage. They had to bid against dealers and collectors who were willing to pay as much as two hundred dollars each for the five hundred pieces which are irreplaceable today; nothing like them remained on the reservations. A Chemehuevi woman remarked that their basketry never had been made for sale, "but for use in this world and the next." She said, "It would never do to bury a Chemehuevi without a basket." (Anonymous 1970d) The items that they were successful in purchasing were for their tribal museum. The Indians' intent was to elicit as much information as possible regarding them from their old people, and to have the collection available for research purposes.

Employment, Housing, and Education

Many of the Indians on the Colorado River Reservation work for the BIA and the U.S. Public Health Service. The latter maintains a fully staffed hospital and field clinic at the agency for the people of the reservation; it can be used by the public in emergencies only. Positions for the Indians include clerks and office workers, carpenters, janitors, bus drivers, cooks, hospital aids, tractor and dragline operators, oilers, truck drivers, surveyors, stakemen, rodmen, engineering aids, ditchriders, mechanics, linemen and groundmen on the power crew, road grader operators, policemen, accountants, teachers, and nurses.

Quarters for the majority of the BIA employees have been furnished at or near the agency, at nominal rentals. They range from very good to poor, but all are equipped with coolers. Living accommodations in Parker are very scarce, and are generally more expensive. Electricity, natural gas, and bottled gas are all available in the area.

The public school system maintains a grammar school and high school in Parker for both Indian and non-Indian children, and a grammar school at Poston, seventeen miles from Parker, for Indian and non-Indian children. The schools are considered very good; they are accredited; and they have good hot lunch programs. Transportation is provided for all pupils living out of town. Very active programs are provided for the youngsters in 4H, FFA, sports, and recreation.

An increasing number of Indian boys and girls from this reservation attend college. Several have won scholarships, and several others are assisted by grants from the tribes or the federal government. These students are said to encounter about the same problems as other college students, and they make about the same grades as average students.

Law Enforcement   Indians and non-Indians cooperate in law enforcement. Offenses committed by non-Indians on the Indian reservations of Arizona are handled by state or county officers exactly as if they had taken place in any non-Indian community. This applies also in most civil cases. Offenses committed by Indians on reservations within Arizona are handled through two courts: (1) if the offense committed is one of the eleven major crimes, it is handled through Federal District Court by the FBI and assistant U.S. Attorney General; (2) if the offense is of the misdemeanor type, the offender is arrested by the tribal policeman or BIA special officer and prosecuted by tribal court. All civil cases wherein the defendant is an Indian and the tort originated on the reservation are handled by tribal courts.

THE YUMAN (QUECHAN) PEOPLE   *Yuma* is said to be an ancient Pima and Papago Indian term for the Indians that comprised one of the oldest groups of the old Yuma-speaking stock. Although commonly called "Yuma Indians," these people actually are *Quechan*, who speak a dialect of the Yuma language. "Quechan" derives from *xam kwatcan*, or "another going down" [on the legendary trail by which they came]. (Johnston 1970:64) Their prehistoric domain "stretched from the Pacific coast in the region of the present international boundary eastward through the mountains, across the southern portion of the less arid south-central valley of California to the Colorado River and beyond into the western portion of the elevated area of Arizona north of the Gila River." (Ezell and Ezell 1970:170) In early historic times they occupied both sides of the Colorado, fifty or sixty miles from the mouth thereof, at and below its junction with the Gila. Fort Yuma was in the approximate center of that territory.

The first explorer to mention the Yuman people by name was Father Kino, in 1701-1702. Later Spanish travelers spoke of them increasingly. They numbered between 3,000 and 3,500. With the treaty of Guadalupe Hidalgo in 1848, most of the Yuma lands passed to the control of the U.S.A.; the Gadsden Purchase

(1853) completed the transfer. Fort Yuma was established and relationships between the Yuma and the whites became close.

The Fort Yuma Reservation   The Fort Yuma Reservation was established by Executive Order of 6 July 1883, amended 9 January 1884, and included approximately 48,608 acres in the reservation proper. Then, on 4 December 1893, through agreement between the Fort Yuma Indians and the U.S.A., all land not considered irrigable was returned to the public domain. Congress ratified that agreement, and the present reservation of 8,661 acres was established. In 1912 the reservation was allotted to the Fort Yuma Indians.

The elevation of the reservation lands varies from one hundred and twenty-five feet along the river to one hundred and forty feet along the All American Canal. On the hill where the subagency headquarters is located, the elevation rises to two hundred and sixty-seven feet above sea level. The land is very good for farming, and it produces high yields when proper practices are followed.

In the Yuma country the climate is very dry, and all farming is done by irrigation. Annual rainfall amounts to approximately three inches, sufficient to support desert flora only. The evaporation rate is very high. Mean annual temperature is 71.9°F. The summers are long and hot, with a maximum temperature of 125°, and the winters are short and mild with a minimum of 22°.

The Quechan have been battling federal authorities on the issues of land and water for many years. Irrigation canals bisect their reservation; they run full of water—into non-Indian hands. One of the Quechan men recently said: "We have a one-inch pipe that brings water into our reservation. At the end of the line, there just is no pressure. We have had to stand by helplessly while several houses there have burned." Despite the ample water in the canals, the Indians cannot get more for their own use. (Mangel 1970:42-43)

Living on the Fort Yuma Reservation are some 1,007 Indians, and an additional 619 enrolled members live off the reservation. As the Quechan Tribe they adopted a constitution and bylaws on 28 November 1936. A council of seven members governs the group; these are elected to office by popular vote.

THE COCOPAH PEOPLE   The Cocopah represent the only remaining group of a series of important Yuman-speaking peoples that occupied the delta of the Colorado River in aboriginal times. All originally dwelt in Mexico—

until the U.S.A. border extended into their territory. The name Cocopah is said to derive from Mohave *Kwi-ka-pah*. (*See* Bahti: 1968:63) They were first mentioned by Europeans about 1605 when they lived in nine rancherías near the river's mouth. These rancherias were inhabited by related people. In 1771 the Cocopah occupied all of the southern one-third of the delta, but four years later they had been pushed to the west side of the river. Garcés reached them in December of 1775. Later, they occupied scattered settlements on both sides of the stream; and in 1900 it was estimated that about six hundred resided on each side, in three major divisions.

Those most favorably located practiced small-scale farming, with corn, beans, black-eyed peas, pumpkins and melons, primarily. Cultivated foods were supplemented by wild ones: seeds, roots and fruits; fish, game and eggs. Nearly all vegetal foods and some fish—derived from the Colorado River and the Gulf of California—were dried and stored for winter. The Cocopah hunted singly on foot, but group hunting came about with the use of horses. Rats and dogs frequently were eaten.

The dwellings were of various types, ranging from thatched temporary structures to more permanent mud-and-wattle houses. Small granaries were constructed with floors elevated above ground.

Until recently shamanism was practiced extensively, primarily for curing the ill. Everything was dream-directed. Women were tattooed and men's features pierced for ornaments; this was believed to be necessary to prevent wandering of the soul after death. Religious activities revolved around death ceremonies, and the dead were cremated. The name of a deceased one was never spoken.

Socially, a loose division of labor was observed. Adult men and women with established families bore the main responsibilities. Men were responsible for the planting, hunting and fishing; women did most of the gathering; and everyone participated in the harvesting. Children had only occasional chores.

Some pottery was made for domestic use, but this industry died out a number of years ago. Loom weaving was practiced and crudely woven cylinders of basketry were made—these were without bottom or top and were set upright on the ground and filled with beans and other items. Shell beads were made to some extent.

The Cocopah engaged to a considerable degree in warfare, mostly of the club and bow and arrow variety. War activities were carried on for hundreds of years, with formalized war patterns and leadership . . . yet the concept of leadership was not expanded to their political and social systems. It has been said that:

Disintegration of Cocopa culture and economy probably began with the disruption of war in the 'fifties, which removed a major field of interest for which, apparently, no substitute was found. Then came the river boats, and an appetite was created for American goods and foods. Finally, after 1900, when the irrigation companies began harnessing the Colorado, the Cocopa served as a source of cheap labor, and a wage economy was inaugurated. During the years between 1905 and 1907, when the Colorado was flowing into the Salton Sea, the Cocopa were left high and dry in their delta habitat. Not only was there no water for their farms, but that same lack prevented the growth of wild plants, and reduced the fish and game supply. It was a question of move or starve. (Kelly, D.S. 1950:167)

Lacking leadership of political, religious, or social nature, their economy and culture declined rapidly. As a people today, the Cocopah are impoverished to an almost unbelievable degree. They live under sub-sub-standard conditions. It is estimated that probably no more than three hundred of them live on each side of the international border. (Johnston 1970:64)

An article written by the senior editor of LOOK (2 June 1970), and factually illustrated, reveals circumstances of the present day Cocopah. Riding along the dirt bank of an irrigation canal, he noted that:

The canal itself, conduit for the valuable water flowing to farmers inland, is neatly cemented and fenced, sharp contrast to the shanties lining its side. The desert grit cuts your eyes and seeps into your mouth and nose even after the car windows roll shut. The kids wipe uselessly at running noses with their sleeves. (Without adequate shelter, clothing, diet or medicine, Indian children remain the number one victims of the respiratory infections that other Americans no longer consider dangerous.) (Mangel 1970:39)

This article is not exaggerated; anthropologists have found conditions to be as set forth here.

The writer described one of the houses as a nine by twelve foot shelter made of flattened cardboard cartons; the six-foot high roof, made of the same materials, was held down by two old automobile tires. Income of the dweller therein was $67.00 a month from welfare. Other residents were found to be living under similar conditions. Cocopah unemployment is cited as "an incredible nine out of ten men."

It was further reported that:

Welfare keeps them alive, with a family income of about $1,000. Among the adolescents, virtually everyone I met had quit school. They desperately seek release from boredom and poverty. Indians have the highest suicide rate in the nation. Two young Cocopah killed themselves the month before I arrived. One was 16, the other, 18. Both had left school years before.

Timidity clouds the Cocopah future. Penniless, disorganized, they are uncertain of their own direction or of where to turn for aid. The BIA, under new and tougher local leadership, is beginning to stir, but slowly. (Ten houses—abandoned when a Marine air base was closed—have been trucked in to one of the three different sites that comprise the Cocopah reservation.) The bedrock problems of schools and job training and employment remain untouched. Cocopah men and women, like Indians elsewhere, are slow to leave the reservations for jobs even if they have the skills and the perseverance to withstand employer prejudice (33 Indian men went to Yuma two years ago to enroll with the Federal employment office; not one has yet been offered a job). The public schools to which most Indian children today are assigned clearly are failing them (eight Indians from one local school attempted junior college in the past few years; none could handle it). (Mangel 1970:41-42)

YUMA CURING SONG

Your heart is good.
[The Spirit] Shining Darkness will be here.
You think only of sad unpleasant things,
You are to think of goodness.
Lie down and sleep here.
Shining Darkness will join us.
You think of this goodness in your dream.
Goodness will be given to you,
I will speak for it, and it will come to pass.
It will happen here,
I will ask for your good,
It will happen as I sit by you,
It will be done as I sit here in this place.

From: *Ethnography of the Yuma Indians*, By C. Daryll Forde

The Cocopah Reservation   An Executive Order of 27 September 1917 established the Cocopah Reservation, setting apart 528 acres for use of the Cocopah Indians; and Public Law 87-150 of 17 August 1961 granted 81 acres of public domain to them. Of the 609 acres, about one hundred are used for small subsistence plots and some for growing cotton. All reservation lands are held by the tribe. Individual plots are assigned for family farms and homesteads. A few of the Cocopah and the Quechan farm for a living, but most of them work for other ranchers or are employed as wage earners in and around the city of

Yuma. Water is currently plentiful, and irrigation water is supplied at a reasonable cost.

Approximately ninety-five Cocopah Indians are enrolled on the Cocopah roster. A number of Cocopah are not eligible for enrollment because of their Mexican birth. Those born in the U.S.A. are citizens and eligible for enrollment. Membership in the tribe and residence on the reservation is open to all Cocopah, whether enrolled or not. Enrollment originally was a matter of individual family choice.

Cocopah government is under the control of a five-member council, elected to office by popular vote. Elections are held in even numbered years on the second Friday in July. The council meets monthly, every second Friday at 1:00 p.m., at Somerton, Arizona.

.... THE PAI

It is said that the native northeasternmost Pai Indians considered themselves as one ethnic group—"the only true human beings on earth," or, in the prevailing notion, "The People." These Pai occupied an area in northwest-central Arizona, "between the Colorado River on the west and north, its Little Colorado tributary on the east, and on the south a line through the San Francisco Peaks, Bill Williams Mountain, Picacho, and down Chino Creek, the Santa Maria River, and Bill Williams Fork." We are told:

These Indians not only spoke a common language but shared a common culture at the time they were first seen by Europeans. During the long period of Spanish and Mexican sovereignty in the Southwest, this group always was designated in Spanish as *Cosninas*, a hispanicized form of the Hopi term for these people, *Ko' ho'-nin* [Cohonina]. The Spaniards, few of whom beside Fray Francisco Garces achieved direct contact with the Pai, preserved the native Indian concept of the "tribal" or cultural unity of this group.

When Anglo-Americans invaded the Southwest and conquered its native peoples, accidents of geographic patterning of their contacts with the Pai led them to conceive of this ethnic group as two "tribes." For a century, therefore, Anglo-Americans have written and thought about "Walapais" and "Havasupais" while the Indians in question continue still to think of themselves as simply Pai. (Dobyns and Euler 1960:49)

"Walapai," or "Hualapai," is said to come from the native Yuman word, *Xawálapáiya*, meaning "pine tree folk." (Swanton 1952:365) It appears that the first mention of them was made in 1776 by Father Garcés, but it is possible that other Spanish explorers encountered them earlier. At any rate, they were never directly affected by the Spaniards. It has been stated that the major effects that Spanish colonization had on the Pai were:

1. an intensification of Pai trade and social intercourse with the Western Pueblos, with a corresponding shift in Pai reference group orientation toward the east, and 2. the beginning of deterioration in some native Pai handicrafts caused by the importation of Spanish goods, which led eventually to substitution of European-made artifacts for native products on a very large scale. In 1776 Garces found the westernmost band of Pai already using Spanish belts, awls, and other implements they had acquired from New Mexico indirectly via Hopi middlemen. (Coues 1900, II:320)

Beginning in 1826, hostilities arose between the Pai and the whites; first with French-Canadian and Anglo-American trappers, and then with slave raiders from the Territory of New Mexico.

About 1842, the Pai, who for some years avoided all possible contacts with the whites, bridled their fear of non-Indian expeditions and began to engage in military actions to preserve their independence and integrity.

After the Southwest was acquired by the U.S.A., a new era of exploration and colonization opened. Captain Lorenzo Sitgreaves, in 1851, encountered eastern Pai bands northeast of Flagstaff, Arizona, and in the upper Truxton Canyon area; and one of his guides (Leroux) was attacked by the Cerbat Mountain Pai band. (Dobyns and Euler 1960:50) Six and seven years later, Lt. E. F. Beale traversed the country of the Pai, and mention was made of a Pai band at Peach Springs, Arizona.

The western bands became known to the federal troops as "Walapai," from the *Hawhala pa'a* band—the one Garcés had noted in 1776. By the close of the War of the Rebellion, "a number of small prospectors' camps were scattered along the western slopes of the Cerbat and Hualapai Mountains where two mining districts had been organized." (Dobyns and Euler 1960:53)

Mining developments, establishment of military posts, and freighting roads wrought increasing changes during the nineteenth century. In 1866, "a typical race-prejudiced frontier type" killed the principal chief of the southern Pai bands. Those bands and the western Pai responded in accord with their time-hallowed traditions and exacted vengeance on the whites, precipitating "the Walapai War". (Dobyns et al. 1957:61)

Unfortunately for the Pai, the western bands went over to the offensive just after the end of the civil conflict in the United States, when men who had found a taste for military life during the war years sought to justify their continued employment in a reduced but still oversized military establishment with far too many senior officers. In the summer of 1867 the river steamers deposited at Fort Mojave contingents of veteran regulars under Lieut. Colonel William Redwood Price to undertake the subjugation of the western Pai bands, labeled "Walapai" and thought of as a tribe.

Lieut. Colonel Price pursued a policy of harrying the elusive western and southern Pai bands as often as possible with the aid of detachments from the post at Fort Whipple, seeking to precipitate a decisive battle. Acutally, the Pai won all the pitched battles fought, choosing their ground carefully, and accepting battle commitment only when they enjoyed equal or superior firepower and superior tactical position behind good rock cover. Price's scorched earth tactics eventually brought the "Walapai" to admit defeat and sue for peace. Effective peace was re-established in 1869, the western and southern Pai admitting Anglo-American military superiority. (U.S. Senate 1936, *in* Dobyns and Euler 1960:53-54)

The social relationship between the conquerers and conquered peoples was yet to be fully clarified, however, for the Pai had still to experience the full range of Anglo-American culture and society. . . .

In 1871 the Pai began to learn that the U.S. Bureau of Indian Affairs considered itself the government agency in charge of administering their transition from native life to subordinate cultural and social status in the United States. A one mile square reservation for the western Pai was set aside in that year.

Committed to the general policy of removing conquered Indians from their ancestral lands to a distinct Indian Territory, the Bureau sought army aid in moving the western Pai to the Colorado River Indian Reservation. The Pai had been placed under the charge of the agent of that reserve in 1873, and in the spring of 1874 the army forcibly moved the western Pai under its direct control to La Paz in the Colorado River Jurisdiction, in the Pai version of the "Long Walk" or "Trail of Tears." The eastern Pai bands, already differentiated from the western groups by pre-contact experiences, safety during the Walapai War, and continued isolation from mines and military posts, were further distinguished from the relocated Pai by their escape from removal. The one or possibly two bands now called Havasupai, the Pine Springs Band, and some of the Peach Springs Canyon Band Pai waited out deportation in the isolated fastnesses of the Grand Canyon and its southern tributaries such as Cataract, National, and Prospect Canyons. (Dobyns and Euler 1960:54-55)

On the low-altitude river flood plain location, the Pai suffered extensively. The government rations on which they were forced to depend were often scarce. Farming had to be attempted under conditions foreign to the experiences of the Pai. Old and young encountered new diseases and died in large numbers. By the spring of 1875, we are told, the decimated bands could take no more; they fled back to their ancestral homeland.

Once safely back in their former territory, the escaped western Pai suffered no illusions as to their fate. They clearly realized that they could not hope to return to their former way of life, because Anglo-American ranchers had thrown great cattle herds onto their grasslands and settled at their best springs. The old harvesting-hunting activities would—and, to the extent they were practiced, did—bring demands by the ranchers for final and irrevocable removal. The western Pai realized that to exist in their homeland they must adopt the white man's expedient of working for wages, and their wholehearted plunge into daily work at the mines gained them the mine operators' support against the antagonistic ranchers, and sealed their differentiation from the still-isolated eastern Pai.

Reservations of lands for the Pai were set aside on the plateau in the prehistoric range of the northeastern bands. The western bands known to Americans as "Walapai" received a 997,045 acre reservation in 1883 . . . and the eastern "Havasupai" group a much smaller plot of 518 acres of its once extensive range in 1882 . . . For nearly half a century neither reservation had much meaning to its theoretical occupants.

Under provisions of the Indian Reorganization Act of June 18, 1934 (48 Stat. 984), separate "tribal" governments were organized on these two jurisdictions, the "Havasupai Tribe" in 1938 and the "Havasupai Tribe" in 1939. (Kelly, Wm. H. 1953:49, 53) By such historic processes and United States administrative actions, arising from a view of the Pai which does not correspond to the native concept, have two formal, self-governing "tribes" been created where only one ethnic group existed in pre-contact times. This process of alienation of Pai bands continues to the present in administrative actions which, for example, send "Havasupai" children to be educated at Indian Bureau boarding schools on the White River Apache reservation while "Walapai" children attend public schools in their homeland. (Dobyns and Euler 1960:55-56)

And thus is explained briefly the circumstances whereby the Yuman-speaking Pai people were divided into the groups which follow.

[It should be noted that while the author generally favors the results of field investigations and thinking of certain scholars (Dobyns and Euler 1960) (Euler 1972b) who feel that both the Hualapai and the Havasupai are directly descendent from the Cerbat branch of the Pai, at least one researcher holds that the Havasupai alone derive from the Cohonina, (Schwartz 1956) and other views are held. (*See* Whiting 1958) (*See* McGregor 1951, 1967) (Schwartz 1959:1062)]

THE HAVASUPAI (EASTERN PAI)

Location and Early History

The eastern Pai, the Havasupai (hah-vah-SOO-pie), or "people of the blue-green water," inhabit a tiny patch of ground at the bottom of Cataract Canyon, a side branch of the Grand Canyon of Arizona. This is within the area occupied by their ancestors since the 1100s at least. During the spring and summer corn, beans, and squash were irrigated with the ever-flowing clear, blue-green water. The crops were supplemented by hunting and gathering over a wide range of altitude. Food stuffs were stored in crevices or small caves above the reach of often occuring flood waters.

Social Organization

At the time of contact with the whites, the Havasupai were a peaceful, industrious, intelligent, and hospitable people. The family was the social unit, with small groups loosely bound into larger ones by blood relationships. No clan existed. Inheritance was in the male line, but wives enjoyed greater privileges and prerogatives than did most women of Arizona Indian peoples. (*See* Robinson 1954:125) No marriage or divorce laws were observed. When young people wished to marry, the man took up residence with the girl's family. They lived with her parents for a year or two, by which time they had a child or two. Then a home was built near that of the man's parents, from whence his inheritance would come. Family association was free of taboos. Women had no share in the house, land, or other property; they owned the pottery, baskets, and their personal effects.

Havasupai homes were rock shelters or houses of two types: One was circular and constructed on a framework of poles. The sidewalls and the domed roof were thatched with bundles of willow branches held in place by small, flexible poles lashed through the thatching to the framework. The other was rectangular and was constructed "by setting four posts in the ground with forks at the top in which poles were laid lengthwise and other poles crosswise, with brush on top ... and the sides thatched with reeds and willow." (Robinson 1954:127) In both instances the roof was covered with earth. No provision was made for the escape of smoke.

Six men of equal status were recognized as "chiefs," and one of them usually served as spokesman and discussion leader. They had little power, their principal duty being to give advice and to lead discussions. Chieftainship was theoretically inherited, but prestige had much to do with the selection. No office of war chief existed; rather the most competent available leader took charge of the rare defensive fighting of the Havasupai.

Religion was little developed. Prayers, in which prayer sticks were utilized, were addressed to the sun, earth, water, rocks and other natural features. The Havasupai believed in a future life and in ghosts. Shamans, or "medicine men," by means of their possession of familiar spirits, dreams, and knowledge of various magical practices, cured diseases and bone fractures, snake bites, and the like, and engaged in weather control.

At some past time the Havasupai are known to have had three dances, but the number decreased. Approximately sixty years ago, a dance of masked and painted men was performed, to bring good fortune and prosperity to the people. The largest celebration came to be a general reunion with dancing which was held annually in the early autumn. Men and women danced in a circle, to the rhythm of drum and voice. Formerly, special attire was worn, but this practice was discarded some time ago. In a measure, the dance was a prayer for rain, but social aspects predominated. Addresses by the chiefs and visitors were given at intervals.

Leisure time was spent in bathing in sweat lodges (small, domed structures about six feet in diameter and four feet high), playing games, playing with dolls, and gossiping—a very general characteristic of Indian peoples. Games included shinny, hoop-and-pole, cup-and-pin, and gambling; wrestling, foot- and horse- racing, and other pursuits were common.

Economy   The Havasupai were successful farmers, and became famous for their crops. In Cataract Canyon, where there was considerable irrigation, corn became the principal crop. Beans, squash, melons, sunflowers, and tobacco also were raised. The men did the irrigating, and the women did most of the harvesting. Plants that were gathered included mescal, cactus and yucca fruits, peaches and figs, mesquite pods, juniper berries, piñones, and the seeds and leaves of several edible vegetal items. Crops were stored in stone granaries which were sealed for protection. Wild honey was collected, and salt was obtained from the Grand Canyon.

Meat was an important part of the diet, as deer, antelope, mountain sheep, wildcat, mountain lion, raccoon, rabbit, and squirrel were hunted. Dogs were used in hunting, but were not eaten. Fish, lizards and other reptiles were not eaten. Men and boys participated in drives to kill rabbits. Other meat came from various rodents. Turkeys, quail, and doves were favorite fowls. Meat was commonly dried. Roasting and boiling were the general methods of cooking. Most of the cooking and eating took place out of doors. Three meals a day were the early practice as well as the modern.

Attire   Clothing of the Havasupai was made from animal skins until recent times—when garments of white man's manufacture came into use. The working of skins and the making of women's clothes was done by the men.

The female attire consisted of a two-part dress—an apron hung from the neck and reaching from breast to ankles in front—and a shorter piece that hung from the waist in back. Under this dress, a short apron was sometimes worn from the waist to the knees. As with the Mohave, the two parts of the dress were overlapped and held in place by tie strings. Around the waist a yucca fiber belt or a textile belt—usually obtained from the Hopi—was worn. Women's clothes had long fringes and were trimmed with metal or hoof tinklers. Later, ornamental shawls made of several colored kerchiefs sewn together also were worn. The moccasins had hard soles and a high upper which was wrapped around the calf. Sometimes the women went barefooted.

Men wore shirts, loincloths, moccasins and leggings. The shirts were similar to those worn by the Plains Indians, but influence of the whites crept in, altering the cut and sewing. The ankle-high moccasins had hard soles. Both men and women wore rabbitskin or cotton blankets for warmth; later they adopted wool blankets.

Face painting and tattooing were practiced to some extent. Adornments consisted of necklaces and ear pendants of Pueblo and Navaho shell and silver. (*See* Douglas 1931:2-3)

Native Crafts   The Havasupai women made pottery which traditionally was fired in an oxidizing atmosphere, like that of the Hopi and other Pueblo pottery makers. The vessels were brown, predominantly globular pots of coarse texture, unslipped and unpainted. They were built up by coiling and then finished by a paddle and anvil process. After being dried in the sun for some twenty-four hours, they were baked, one by one, in hot coals.

Basketry was made by the women following two techniques, coiling and twining. Training in the craft began when a girl was seven or eight years old. Shallow trays or bowls were coiled, using twigs of cottonwood or of a plant said to be known only by its Havasupai name. The sewing of the coils was on a three-rod foundation. Simple geometric and banded designs were worked in martynia black. Conical burden baskets, globular water jugs, and shallow trays or bowls were made by twining. For these, twigs of acacia were preferred, although cottonwood and willow also were used. Some of the baskets were used as cooking containers.

The burden baskets and water jugs had loops for carrying; these baskets were decorated with simple designs achieved by varieties of twining and the use of martynia, or devil's claw. Designs were generally poorly executed. The water vessels and some parching trays were coated with a yucca, or soapweed, paste colored red with hematite, over which a coating of piñon gum was applied for waterproofing. This resulted in almost completely obscuring the designs.

In weave, the old Havasupai baskets displayed some similarity to those of the Yavapai, but not those of the Walapai. Today, Havasupai baskets are extremely rare. Those made in recent times are of coil technique, and made primarily for the tourist trade.

Havasupai babies were placed on basketry cradleboards, and kept there until they were nearly old enough to walk. Care of the children was shared by both parents.

Trade   The Havasupai and their kinsmen, the Hualapai, both of whom were great traders, widely traded seashells from the Pacific and red hematite (for paint) to the Pueblo peoples.

Significantly, the historic trade routes had similar or identical prehistoric counterparts; these are indicated by a wide distribution of trade items. (*See* Colton 1941) We are told that lima beans, for which the Hopi have become well known, apparently were obtained originally from the Havasupai; and the latter received peaches from the Hopi. "Some Havasupai lived with the Hopi regularly, during the winter months, for a period of years." (Whiting 1958:58) For grinding purposes the Havasupai used a flat pounding-grinding rock and rotary mortars.

Impacts of
Foreign Culture   The period of peaceful stability of the Havasupai ended near A.D. 1600, with the first impacts of foreign culture. As the whites moved onto the uplands for cattle ranching, the territory of the Indians was gradually usurped. Most of the aboriginal articles were still being made: pottery in paddle and anvil technique, clay pipes for smoking, stone knives (which among other uses, were utilized for cutting up squash), bone tools, fire drills and hearths, bows and arrows, basketry, skin clothing, and related items. Three main architectural forms persisted: a brush structure (wickiup), the rock shelter, and a talus top granary. Many old customs, such as cremation, persisted. (*See* Schwartz 1956:83; *see also* Whiting 1958:58)

The historic Havasupai were individualists in their economic pursuits, their house types, and in their lack of well organized social or religious groups. It has been stated that:

While at times they borrowed extensively from the Hopi in economic and religious matters they remained reluctant farmers (especially after there were horses to ride or, better still, to race), indifferent craftsmen, inartistic, nonreligious and magnificently self-sustaining people. The dead, who were greatly feared, were socially ostracized and physically buried at a considerable distance from the living areas. The mode of burial varied. (Whiting 1958:56)

Upon death, the home and personal possessions were burned, and one or more horses killed on the grave. A man's saddle might be burned, or left on one of the horses. (*See* Dobyns and Euler 1971:44) His bow and arrows, war club, and personal effects were buried with him.

Modernization   Havasupai acculturation really began with the establishment of a reservation for them in 1880. Toward the end of the following decade, the federal government sent a farmer into the canyon, and then a schoolteacher. New and improved tools, modern methods, and the English language were introduced. The school forced the children to remain in the canyon. Clothing rapidly changed to the white man's garb, western style. The typical burial practice of cremation was altered to burial directly in the ground, (Whiting 1958:56) in extended position, although for another generation "there continued to be cremations, often of the medicine men. There is some hint that these men, ultra-individualistic in life, demanded to be different in death, no matter what the current pattern. Even in their treatment of new ideas this group behaved as an almost accidental amalgamation of individuals." Mourning rites of the Yuman type prevailed in the Havasupai culture.

Despite the fact that the Havasupai borrowed extensively from the Hopi at times, the rituals in imitation of the Hopi katsina dances "were strictly individually sponsored affairs. When the sponsoring individual died or when his proposed reform failed, as when prayers for rain were answered with a disastrous flood, the movement evaporated." (Whiting 1958:56)

A big flood in the Havasu canyon in 1910 washed out most of the farms and homes there and the talus top granaries, after which small wooden frame houses were erected, along with rebuilding of the brush shelters. For a time the Havasupai, like many other Indian peoples when initially confronted with non-traditional types of dwellings, used the frame houses for storage purposes while preferring to live in the old style homes.

The National Park Service established a village near the Grand Canyon Park settlement on the plateau, which came to be a center of Havasupai life. Most of the Indians work for the Park Service or for some non-Indian concerns engaged in servicing the park and visitors. Some eke out a meager living by growing garden crops and raising a few cattle.

The Havasupai Reservation   Certain lands in Arizona were reserved by an Executive Order of 8 June 1880 for the "Suppai" Indians. That order was revoked by another of 23 November 1880, which set aside other lands; that in turn was revoked on 31 March 1882, at which time still other lands were reserved for the "Yavai Suppai" Indians. The reservation itself consists of 518 acres, which are owned in undivided shares by the enrolled members.

The Havasupai lost their eastern fields and hunting and grazing lands on the plateau above the canyons, (*see* Dobyns and Euler 1971:21-24, 30-33) and now have use of only a few square miles. The U.S. Forest Service and the NPS issue a year-to-year permit for the Havasupai to graze their stock on land adjacent to the reservation in the Kaibab National Forest and the park.

The beauty and isolation of Cataract Canyon—now commonly called the Havasu—long have been the root resource of the Havasupai. Homes, school and other facilities could be reached only by trails on either side of the canyon, which cuts through the reservation. These are accessible by roads from the Grand Canyon and from Highway 66, just east of Peach Springs, Arizona. Horse and mule transportation and guide service are provided by the Indians, and overnight accommodations at Supai Village, a little oasis. Airlift by helicopter is available for visitors (at $120 per hour), but the Indians in need of supplies must travel to Kingman, one hundred miles from their homes. From there, it is said that merchants will ship goods back to the canyon at a 40 to 60 per cent premium. (Anonymous 1969c:21*)

The Havasupai Tribe   The Havasupai organized under a constitution and bylaws which were approved on 27 March 1939. A tribal corporate charter was ratified on 5 October 1946.

All individuals listed on tribal rolls as of 1938 are members. New members are added as follows: (1) all children born to any member after January 1, 1938, who are three-fourths or more Indian blood, and (2) by action of the Tribal Council through the passage of ordinances covering future membership and adoption of new members, subject to the approval of the Secretary of the Interior. No person is eligible for adoption into the Hualapai (*sic.*) [Havasupai?] Tribe who has not resided upon the reservation for a probationary period of five years. (Kelly, Wm. H. 1953:55)

The Havasupai now number about 500. The population is predominantly young, with rising birth rate. (*See* Dobyns and Euler 1971:1, 61-62) As a people, the Havasupai have moved from

*Information from *Time, The Weekly Newsmagazine.*

traditional practices toward modern government in a practical manner. It was recorded that: "The governing body is a tribal council consisting of four regular councilmen, and three recognized hereditary chiefs of the tribe who are selected by the remaining subchiefs. Each of the chiefs, as a regular member of the Council, continues his duties as councilman until death or resignation, at which time a new chief is selected by the subchiefs. Any member of the Council, not a chief, may be subject to recall if he fails to fulfill his duties as a councilman . . ." (Kelly, Wm. H. 1953:55) Today all members of the council are elected.

The Havasupai Tribal Council meets once each month at the Community Building in Supai. All members of the council must be qualified voters of the reservation and thirty-five years of age or over. Elections are held every two years on 25 December. Tribal officers and tribal employees are selected by the council. The chairman and vice-chairman must be members of the council, but the secretary and treasurer may be from within or without the membership of the council. Officers also include a tribal judge and police chief. Currently, the council has seven members; men or women may serve. Special meetings are at the call of the chairman. The Havasupai have five operating committees under their chairmen who are listed as Store Manager, Assistant Manager, General Manager, Community Action Program, and Tourist Director.

Education is provided by the BIA in Supai, for those in the pre-primary through fourth or fifth grades—depending upon the need. Thereafter, students are sent to school in Fort Apache or in Phoenix. The nearest professional medical care available is at the Grand Canyon.

The Havasupai Today   By national standards, the Havasupai are considered among the most impoverished groups in the nation. They are almost totally dependent on the BIA.

It recently has been said that:

Young Havasupai who attend Government boarding schools return to the reservation confused about their place in the world. They feel inferior both to the white man [*haigu*] and to fellow Indians from larger, more advanced tribes.

Of the 142 Havasupai men able to work, only eight hold permanent jobs. While the tourist season lasts, the tribe's 300 horses are used to pack visitors to the canyon (at $16 a round trip). Some 6,000 came by foot or horseback last year, but the tribe has almost nothing in the way of handicrafted goods, restaurants or inns that might encourage visitors to leave their money behind. Moreover, the horses help to keep the tribe isolated. Efforts to put a cable car line or jeep trail into Supai have been resisted by the Indians, who fear that their only reliable source of income will be destroyed.

Havasupai are forbidden to bring alcohol onto the reservation, but it is bootlegged into the canyon and sold at exorbitant prices. Increasingly, the younger tribe members have been the best customers . . . .

The Havasupai family structure may appear to be almost nonexistent. But this is not the case. Actually, the family is extremely important; "it is the most important institution (after the BIA) in the community." (Martin 1972)

It has been noted that:

Without privacy, children imitate their elders and begin sexual activity early. Illegitimacy is rampant, birth control ignored. Havasupai men ... practice "sequential marriages," (Martin 1972) taking one wife after another. Matches between first cousins are routine; mental retardation is common [evidence to support this statement is questioned]. (Euler 1972b) Disease, poor diet and high infant mortality combine to give the Havasupai a life expectancy of only 44 years (U.S. average 70). They also have a suicide rate 15% above the national average. (Anonymous 1969c:21*)

During the summer of 1969, a government-financed airlift set about to bring modern housing to the isolated Havasupai Indians in Havasu canyon. Helicopters, in some eighty flights, lowered five prefabricated, three-bedroom houses, section by section, to the canyon floor 5,300 feet below the rim for the Indians to erect. These structures cost about $12,000 each. They were provided at random for some of the most needy families. Later, ten more houses were put up in Supai, and thirty-five were scheduled for installation.

As in prior times, the Indians had to be talked into accepting the new houses. They knew their neighbors would be antagonistic and jealous; and the dwellings, although wired for electricity, had no source of power. The wood stoves that were supplied would be sources of trouble in an area where a firewood shortage prevails . . . and so the houses would be impossible to heat.

An official of the BIA said that the Agency planned to provide each Havasupai family with a modern house eventually, thus replacing the sub-standard shacks, many without floors. (Anonymous 1969a)

The writer of the article quoted above remarked:

*Reprinted by permission from *Time, The Weekly Newsmagazine;* Copyright Time, Inc.

Until now, the Bureau of Indian Affairs has invested only limited funds and manpower to ease the tribe's plight. Little in the way of imaginative social work has been attempted. Putting shingled rooftops over each Havasupai's head is a questionable response to his needs, and even this will be done only gradually. (Anonymous 1969c:21*)

Construction of houses, a community building and federal facilities, with supplemental work, and employment at the power plant provided an unusual "bonanza" for the workers. However, this will end "and the Havasupai will then be thrown back on tourism and welfare." (Martin 1972)

HAVASUPAI PRAYER

Sun, my relative
Be good coming out
Do something good for us.

Make me work,
So I can do anything in the garden
I hoe, I plant corn, I irrigate.

You, sun, be good going down at sunset
We lay down to sleep I want to feel good.

While I sleep you come up.
Go on your course many times.
Make good things for us men.

Make me always the same as I am now.

From: *Havasupai Ethnography*, by Leslie Spier (1928:226)

HUALAPAI, OR WALAPAI (WESTERN PAI)

Anciently, the western Pai, or Hualapai, appear to have occupied territory between present day Kingman, Arizona, and the Colorado River. Around A.D. 1150, the Cerbat group moved onto the plateau east of the Grand Wash Cliffs, where they displaced the Cohonina people. Their closest contacts were with the Yuman-speaking Halchidhoma, and the Southern Pai and Hopi peoples. (Euler 1972b) They had hostile encounters with the Yavapai. Before 1880 the Hualapai probably numbered more than 1,000, but they declined steadily to the present.

A major occupation was food gathering and hunting; vegetal products were primary, for game was limited. The main food supply consisted of fruits, berries, and nuts gathered by the women, and deer, antelope, mountain sheep, rabbits, and other game hunted by the men. Farming was practiced where moisture was sufficient to raise crops, as in many canyons tributary to the Colorado. In western Grand Canyon the Hualapai practiced agriculture as extensively as did the Havasupai in Cataract Canyon.

Dwellings commonly were small, not very substantial structures of dome-shape, made of small poles and branches covered with juniper bark or thatched and without earth covering. Sturdier winter houses were sometimes built. Rock shelters were often places of abode. Sweat houses were in common use, and a rectangular, flat-roofed shelter was built occasionally for summer shade.

Few ceremonies or dances were held, although the Pai traditionally had great faith in shamanism—usually in the hands of a medical practitioner. Some are said to believe that the spirit of the dead goes to the west for judgment and, if condemned, goes to the underworld; others have no concept of future life. In times past, the dead were cremated and their possessions burned. An annual community burning of food and clothing commemorated the dead. Cremation was replaced by the practice of burial—preferably at the place of birth.

Basketry was made exclusively by the Hualapai women. They fashioned undecorated plaques and household baskets, often covered with pitch on the interior; more or less cylindrical baskets with geometric designs in martynia, rarely painted bluish, red or white on the outside, and similarly shaped with bail-like handles; large conical carrying baskets with limited decoration; finely worked small plaques, the splints of which were dyed; baby cradles and items of fanciful shapes. The weaving technique is that of coil on three rods and splint foundation; and the products resemble those of the Apache. In time, the basketry art almost died out, but tourist demands caused its continuance to the present. The modern baskets are made of sumac twigs and in brighter colors; predominantly of bowl shape. Some beadwork is also produced for the tourist trade. Formerly, some pottery and pottery pipes were made. Tobacco grew wild in the Hualapai country; it was not cultivated. (Robinson 1954:117)

The Hualapai Indian Reservation

Rugged and varied terrain lies between Peach Springs, Arizona, on U.S. Highway 66, and the Colorado River west of Grand Canyon National Park. This relatively large reservation has only a few tillable spots near streams and springs. Small crops such as corn and beans may be raised, but the chief means of livelihood is by stockraising, while the most profitable source of income is from the sale of timber, which is treated as a capital asset with the return invested in range improvement.

The reservation in its entirety is owned in undivided shares by the enrolled Indians, and is held in trust for them by the federal government. Consolidation of the reservation was accomplished in 1947, when title to more than 500,000 acres in odd numbered sections previously held by the Santa Fe Railroad Company was quieted in the government in trust for the Hualapai. (*See* Kelly Wm. H. 1953:50) The land is used for individual homes and farms, for grazing by their cattle association, and by the Indians acting as a corporation.

The Hualapai Trading Company at Peach Springs was established in 1944 by the "tribe," for the purpose of providing a local source of groceries and other merchandise, with credit privileges. All cattle on the reservation are owned by members of the Hualapai Livestock Association, with exception of the tribal herd.

The Hualapai Tribe

This group of Indians was organized as the Hualapai Tribe, with a constitution and bylaws approved 17 December 1938; and a corporate charter was ratified on 5 June 1943. All individuals listed on the rolls as of 1938 are members, and children born to any member after 1 January 1938, who are of one-half degree or more Indian blood, are also members. Others admitted by action of the tribal council "through the passage of ordinances, subject to the approval of the Secretary of the Interior, governing future membership and adoption of new members" may be added to the rolls. The local population is now about 685.

The tribal council consists of eight members, in addition to "one hereditary chief of the tribe selected by the subchiefs of the various recognized bands and who holds office for life." Councilmen must be qualified voters of twenty-five years or more of age, members of the Hualapai tribe, and residents of the reservation. All tribal officers, committees and tribal employees are selected by the council. Council officers consist of a chairman and vice-chairman, secretary, treasurer, judge, and police chief; the first two named must be members of the council, but others may be chosen from the tribe as a whole.

As to their responsibilities:

The Hualapai Tribal Council has jurisdiction over all matters pertaining to the management of tribal property, conduct of Indians and non-Indians on the reservation, tribal business enterprises, and the welfare of tribal members. The only limits to its power are in some specific instances where the Secretary of the Interior must give approval for action, and in other instances where action must be referred to a vote of the people. (*See* Kelly, Wm. H. 1953:49)

The group has committees, each with a chairman, which give attention to Budget and Finance; Constitution and Bylaws; Health, Education and Welfare; Law and Order, Recreation, Community Action Program and Administration Board, Northwest Planning Area, and the Tribal Herd.

The Hualapai received $2.9 million compensation for lands taken from them in northwestern Arizona in 1883. They decided to use 25 per cent of this fund for a program to better their standard of living, and 75 per cent for resources development and investment programs. (Anonymous 1970e)

The council meets the first Saturday of each month at 9:00 a.m. in the tribal office in Peach Springs. Terms of office are for three years, with elections held annually on the first Saturday in June.

Children that live on the reservation attend the Indian Service day school at Peach Springs and the public schools in Kingman, Truxton Canyon, and Seligman, or go to off-reservation boarding schools. Almost without exception, the people speak English; many retain their native tongue. The Hualapai have a PHS clinic in Peach Springs, where a medical doctor, several nurses and other personnel are assigned. Ambulance service is provided where necessary for those requiring hospitalization, as in the Kingman Hospital.

The Hualapai at Big Sandy Some years past, a few members of the Hualapai tribe lived at Big Sandy, southeast of Kingman. But, by 1963-1964 all that remained was "one shack, some fields, fences and the irrigation ditches . . . . the 'owners,' who were many, lived in Kingman. Several commuted to plant, irrigate, weed and harvest some small kitchen gardens." (Martin 1972) No tribal land exists in the Big Sandy; all tracts are held in trust allotments. Mohave county assumes responsibility for Law and Order.

Fig. 1   The *Tcirkwena*, or Skipping Dance. From the San
Xavier district of the Papago Reservation.

Photo by James Griffith

Fig. 2   Scene in Papaguera. Papago Indian cowboys cut out horses in one of their corrals built of mesquite poles.

Photo courtesy BIA, Branch of Land Operations,
SMC Cartographic Section, Concho, Oklahoma

Fig. 3   A lettuce harvest on the Colorado River Indian Reservation.

Photo courtesy BIA, Branch of Land Operations,
SMC Cartographic Section, Concho, Oklahoma

Fig. 4 A Papago woman puts tamales into a steaming pot. The structure in the background is an earthen oven in which the bread is baked when many are to be fed.

Photo by Earl de Berg (1971)

Fig. 5 A Mohave effigy jar.

Photo by Leslie Buckland

THE SALT RIVER INDIAN AGENCY

The Salt River Agency was given full status as of 1 July 1962. Prior to that time it functioned as a sub-agency of the Pima Indian Agency located at Sacaton, fifty miles distant. It now administers the affairs of Indians living in the Salt River Pima-Maricopa community and the Fort McDowell Yavapai-Apache community. The agency headquarters is located in Maricopa county, about seven miles east of Phoenix, Arizona, between Scottsdale and Mesa on McDowell Road. Its purpose is to provide facilities for the education, assistance and guidance of the Indian residents of these lands, "so that they may become more self-sufficient, may improve their social and economic status, and develop and protect their natural resources." (King 1967)

THE SALT RIVER RESERVATION This reservation was established by Act of Congress on 28 February 1859, and by subsequent executive orders. It begins approximately two miles northeast of Tempe and extends up the Salt River past the Granite Reef diversion dam and beyond the junction with the Verde River. On the west the reservation approaches Scottsdale. The reservation contains 45,627 acres of which 25,229 acres are trust allotted to individual Indians in tracts of five to 30 acres; and 21,398 acres are community land. Forage on range lands is undependable. Carrying capacity is rated at 145 head of cattle. Vegetation includes sahuaro, mesquite, palo verde, cat-claw, cacti, creosote bush, salt cedar, and arrowweed. Animal life consists primarily of jackrabbit and cottontail, mourning and whitewing dove, gopher, muskrat, desert beaver, and quail.

Virtually all of 15,000 acres of irrigated land is leased to non-Indian farmers who have developed a successful agricultural project. Valuable water rights go with the lands in this project.

The irrigated area on the west side of the reservation is the center of the Indian community, with the remainder of the reservation practically vacant of human habitation.

Flat desert land to the north and east could be subjugated for agriculture if sufficient water were available. To the east, the reservation is made up of rolling desert, some of spectacular beauty, rising into rocky prominences.

The average elevation of the cultivated lands is approximately

1300 feet; the highest point in the reservation is Mount McDowell which rises to 2828 feet. The winters are mild but killing frosts may occur from November to March. Moderate rains fall from December to April and thunder storms may appear in July, August and September; the average annual rainfall is 7.96 inches. The summers are hot, the temperature ranging from 115° to 31°, and averaging about 70.2°F. Relative humidity is generally low.

THE PIMA-MARICOPA COMMUNITY

Some 1,700 Pima-Maricopa people representing about 330 families live in the Salt River community, which was organized under the Wheeler-Howard Act, with a constitution and bylaws approved 11 June 1940. These people are descendants of Pima and Maricopa bands that migrated to the area beginning in the 1860's when the waters in the Gila River failed. A minority of Papago and Indians of other tribes have married into the community. An additional 300 tribal members live immediately adjacent to the reservation. The clothing worn is that of the regional inhabitants.

A tribal council of seven members is active, with a president and vice-president appointed from within the popularly elected council membership; other officers are a secretary, treasurer, tribal judge and police chief. Elections are held every other year, the last week in June. The community has its own Law and Order Code. Real leadership is being developed within the community, several committees operate effectively, and governmental pursuits are expanding. The council meets each Thursday at 4:30 p.m., at the Community Center.

Compared with some of the other Arizona Indians, the Pima-Maricopa are relatively well educated; almost all persons under the age of fifty years have at least a sixth grade education. Just under 15 per cent have completed high school. Virtually everyone speaks English. Despite these facts, the economic conditions on the reservation have not been good. A significant percentage of the work force is unemployed or works intermittently. Urbanization has robbed the Indians of the traditional agricultural activities in which they were experienced. Some basketry is woven; in fact a revival of the craft is underway, with younger Indian women and some non-Indians learning to weave in the traditional manner.

Because the community is in an area which is one of the largest winter tourist resort centers in the nation, future development is a certainty. Industry is getting a foothold in the area, increasing the population and economy throughout the Salt River valley. The Indians will relate to future developments. A program to upgrade the reservation's work force through vocational training is under way, and a program of social development of the Indian community is being pushed.

Among the projects being advanced are those of self-help housing, improved domestic water under the U.S. Public Health Service, establishment of a large Community Center—where an annual Indian Trade Fair has been held since the spring of 1962—and various youth programs. To aid in achieving these objectives, the agency staff has been expanded to include a resources development officer, a juvenile officer, and a graduate social worker.

An elementary school is operated by the BIA on the reservation. And a contract with the state of Arizona provides for education of Indian children in both elementary and high school. Educational grants are sought for higher education. Indian languages are heard but little now, and in another generation it is expected they will be entirely replaced by English—unless interest in native tongues is rekindled.

THE YAVAPAI INDIANS

The Yavapai (YAH-vah-pie) are a Yuman-speaking group which the Mohave called the "People of the Sun" (*Enyaéva*—"sun"; *pai*—"The People"). They were first mentioned by Espejo in 1582.) They wandered in small independent bands or family groups over the semi-desert reaches bounded by the mountains generally north of the Gila River. Their number is said not to have exceeded 1,500. (Robinson 1954:84) These groups occupied three geographical districts, comprising the western, northeastern, and southeastern Yavapai respectively. They intermingled and intermarried. Leadership was achieved through personal merit based on wisdom, personality and ability as a warrior. (Robinson 1954:85)

Until the late 1800's, Yavapai subsistence was derived from hunting small animals, rabbits and deer (they used a recurved bow), and the gathering of native plants; occasionally corn was obtained from the Pima and Papago Indians. They were active traders and participated in expeditions to the west coast, south into Mexico, north to the Paiute country, and to the Hopi and Zuñi pueblos. They were important factors in the exchange of handiworks and in the mingling of the cultures of the diverse Indians they visited.

The Yavapai made use of caves for shelter, or built temporary pole, brush, and mud houses. Small quantities of corn were planted along stream bottomlands, but the yield was not sufficient to be counted as a staple food. A variety of fine baskets was woven for utilitarian purposes, (*See* Robinson 1954:79-84) and a few stone tools were used. Food appears to have been cooked in pottery vessels. The clothing, if worn, was made from hides; personal adornments were few. Small crosses were sometimes tied to the hair.

Their religion was like that of most other Yuman peoples. Prominent features were veneration of the sun, shamanism, and belief in dream omens. Social dances were held on occasion.

The Yavapai were long associated with the Apache, and writers have often confused them. Both being warlike, the Yavapai found it to their advantage to be associated with the Apache. They intermingled and intermarried to some extent, and were similar in attire and even physical appearance. Here the similarities ended. The Apache, of Athabascan stock, assumed an attitude of warfare against all those regarded as outsiders, while the Yavapai philosophy permitted more flexibility. They demonstrated a greater willingness to change and, in time, made the effort to learn the ways of their neighbors and to coexist with them.

General Crook was one who did not recognize the Yavapai as a people apart from the Apache—to him they were one and the same, all Apache. (*See* Robinson 1954:91) In 1872 some 750 Indians—mostly Yavapai—were living on a reservation at Camp Date Creek, southwest of present day Prescott. The surgeon there, Dr. Corbusier, was one of those more discerning than Crook and recognized the difference between the Yavapai and the Apache. However, the next year, in May, they were all transferred to the Camp Verde Reservation which had been established in 1871. Many Indians escaped from there, some of them to resume raiding the settlers of Arizona and Mexico. After an extensive campaign in April, 1873, the Yavapai, Hualapai (eastern Pai), and Tonto submitted to armed forces, or were brought in the following year. At that time the San Carlos Reservation was established, and the Yavapai, being identified as Apache, were forced to go there. It has been recorded that:

The Indians walked all the way while the soldiers rode ponies. They followed only trails, for there were no roads. Moccasins and clothes wore out, torn by rocks, cactus, and brush, and many, sick at heart, wanted to die—and did. With no time for burial, these were left lying along the way. Many streams and a large river running high were crossed. These were negotiated the best way they could, one way or another. Some of the weaker were lost at the river crossing.

Rations were meager, and were augmented by edible weeds, roots, and seeds, when they could be found. To the Yavapai Indians, this move is known as the "March of Tears." . . .

During the next several years, many of the Yavapai drifted away from the San Carlos Reservation and went to live in the area north and west of Fort Whipple and the Verde. The four branches of the Yavapai Indians and their area headquarters may be said to be divided as follows: "Weepukapa" (Camp Verde); "Tolkepaya" (Arlington); "Kewevkopaya" (Fort McDowell); and "Yavepe" (Prescott) [in the spelling "Yawape," this term is said to mean "crooked mouth people," or "sulky"]. (Bahti 1968:68) The Arlington branch has practically disappeared, the remaining members having been absorbed into the Prescott and Fort McDowell branches. (Barnett 1968:3-4)

It has been said that the older Yavapai women taught the Apache to make bowls and dishes, and also improved coiled basket making techniques while they were together at San Carlos from 1875-1900. The two peoples spent many hours working together, thus accounting for the materials, techniques, and many decorative designs that are found in the baskets of both. However, the Apache lacked legend or background for their craft. (Robinson 1954:78-84)

It is pointed out that:

Many design elements, such as the diamond for example, are claimed by the Yavapai weavers as originating with their tribe. The star (starflower) design is common in Yavapai baskets, and is a sacred symbol with the weavers. Some, but not all, of the best baskets begin with the design of the story of creation. The swastika is a mystic symbol of good luck to the Indian, and brings good fortune when used on baskets, pottery and blankets. It is believed by the Indians that this symbol was given to them by the Great Spirit.

No dye or artificial color is used in a Yavapai basket. Young shoots of cottonwood and mulberry trees, and sometimes the fine roots of the yucca or soapweed are used for the natural color. The black color is made from stripped ears of the devil's claw seed pods. Generally the first coil of a Yavapai basket is black, though some weavers do not always hold to this. (Barnett 1968:33)

To finish a basket, the last row of weaving—the rim as it were—is always done in black. Yavapai baskets are now extremely rare; only a few women can make them.

THE YAVAPAI-APACHE AND MOHAVE-APACHE
The Fort McDowell Reservation

Originally this was established as Camp McDowell Military Reserve on 1 January 1873. It was released to the Department of the Interior on 1 February 1891 for disposal under government procedures (Acts of 5 July 1884 and 23 August 1894), reserving legal subdivisions occupied by government improvements. Some of the land subsequently was taken up by white settlers.

In November, 1901, the Federal Land Office was directed to reserve the land for Indian purposes; and an Executive Order of 15 September 1903 set aside the land of Camp McDowell that was not legally settled. Purchases and the Act of 2 April 1904 compensated the settlers for their improvements and claims, thus changing all of Camp McDowell to an Indian reservation.

Most of the present inhabitants of Fort McDowell are descendants of those Yavapai who were taken as prisoners to San Carlos in 1874-1875. They are related to and acquainted with Yavapai living in the Camp Verde vicinity and at Prescott. At the time of imprisonment the Yavapai numbered approximately 1,500; twenty-five years later only 200 remained. (Barnett 1968:4)

A limited number of Apache have intermarried with the Fort McDowell Yavapai, or "Mohave-Apache"—as they were called erroneously by the early whites—and live on the Fort McDowell Reservation.

It is located twenty-eight miles northeast of Phoenix, and adjoining the Salt River Reservation on the northeast side. It contains 24,680 acres, none of which is allotted. Total length of the reservation is ten miles, and its four-mile width is bisected lengthwise by the Verde River, beginning one and a half miles above the junction with the Salt River. The elevation of the bottomland varies from 1,350 to 1,900 feet. Some 1,300 acres of irrigable lands of the Fort McDowell Reservation were provided water by rights granted by the Kent Decree in 1910.

The climate in which the Indians reside, that of the Southwest arid region in general, is somewhat modified by proximity to the mountains. Winters although mild do experience some moderate frosts, a little snow, and limited rains from December to April. The summers are long, hot and dry, with thunderstorms in July, August, and September. Temperature during the year varies from a recorded high of 115° to a low of 13° and averages about 70°F. The annual rainfall is ten inches. Heavy clothing is seldom needed.

On 3 March 1965, the Indian Claims Commission ruled that the Fort McDowell Reservation was part of 9,238,600 acres of Yavapai tribal land confiscated by the U.S. government on 1 May 1873. This meant that the Indians owned the land all the time, and in 1904 were getting only what had been theirs all along. Following this ruling, the federal government paid the Indians $5,100,000 for the Yavapai tribal lands that had been taken—the settlement amounting to about fifty-three cents an acre!

This reservation became important to the Central Arizona Project, or CAP, because of the need for storage reservoirs. The project is supposed to help the state of Arizona, but it will put about half of the Fort McDowell Reservation lands in flood danger, and will force the Indians living there either to relocate their homes or live within the shadow of possible disaster, because practically all of the residences are located in the flood plain.

According to a report in *The Arizona Republic*:

When the CAP bill was passed, it included the construction of Orme Dam, either at the confluence of the Salt and Verde Rivers or at Granite Reef Dam a short distance to the south.

In either case, the dam will create a flood plain of 12,823 acres along the always-flowing Verde River, which runs through the middle of the reservation.

The flood plain boundary is based on the biggest flood of the last 100 years, and much of the land might not be inundated for several generations. But there will always loom the possibility that the 100 year flood might strike again tomorrow.

Land in the flood plain can be used for farming and grazing and other purposes, but construction of the permanent structures will be restricted.

Within the flood plain will be . . . 5,347 acres near the river designated as the "conservation pool," or the mud flats. Water will be backed into this area when the reservoirs are fullest during a normal year's runoff.

The federal government, meanwhile, is willing to help the Indians relocate their small village, Ft. McDowell, and to reimburse the tribe for the land in the flood plain. Also, the CAP bill provided for the gift of 2,500 acres in federal lands to the tribe. This land will probably come from nearby Forest Service lands.

But the tribe is sometimes suspicious of the way the federal government operates. For example, the tribe thought the government would set aside comparable land east of the reservation to trade for the property in the flood plain.

However, the government recently traded that land to the Page Land and Cattle Co. for land elsewhere. Now, according to a former tribal chairman the Indians have no place to get the kind of terrain they are giving up.

The chairman said that the Indians are reasonable people and that they recognize the importance of the CAP. In speaking of the federal government, however, he remarked: "They took away 9 million acres from us; then they said we'll give you this 24,000 acres and let you alone. Now they want to take half of that. My

people are starting to think that they won't stand by their word."
(Murray 1969)

The Yavapai here number approximately 57 families, totaling about 300 persons. Most of the people live in board houses; a few have cinder block dwellings, chiefly built under a self-help program. They have their own government with elected council members and working committees. Both men and women hold offices. The Fort McDowell Council meets at 2:00 p.m., on the first Tuesday of each month, in the Community Building in Fort McDowell. Elections are held every year; officers are a chairman, vice-chairman, secretary, and police chief. Law enforcement is subject to Title 25 of the U.S. Code. Tribal policemen have jurisdiction over misdemeanors committed on the reservation by Indians.

Little farming is underway currently, and the principal source of income is from wages paid to tribal members as employees in pumping stations of the city water system of Phoenix. About 15 per cent commute to off-reservation employment. The sale of permits for duck hunting, fishing, and picnicking provides a small income for the tribe. The lands along the Verde River offer a considerable potential for development as a recreational area, should such be undertaken.

Presently, most recreational facilities have to be sought in surrounding towns, such as Phoenix, Mesa, Tempe, and Scottsdale. There, too, the shopping is done, and medical and dental services secured. Churches of most denominations are available. Arizona State University at Tempe is about ten miles from the agency headquarters. A few of the younger Yavapai are college graduates.

The pressures inherent in the accelerated growth of the surrounding cities continue to mount as those communities enlarge on the periphery of the Salt River Reservation and the Fort McDowell Reservation. Both tribal groups are engaged in such studies and community redevelopment activities as may best assure them of a meaningful place in the future of the valley. Maximum coordination with the surrounding communities in developmental planning is believed to have assured a mutually advantageous future.

Viable tribal housing and sanitation programs are in operation. Modern building codes and ordinances have been adopted and all educational and developmental opportunities offered through the OEO and other federal sources are being utilized to the fullest by the tribal councils.

Annual income from leases, licenses, fees and recreation

receipts approximate $76,000 for the Fort McDowell group, and $300,000 for the Salt River community.

Both of these groups have coordinated their athletic and entertainment programs with those of the surrounding communities. No special Indian-type tourist shows are held.

One criminal investigator is employed at the agency. He is charged with the responsibility of maintaining law and order on these two reservations; he drives a police car equipped with a two-way radio. Radio contact is maintained with the Pinal and Maricopa county sheriffs' offices, and messages can be relayed to police in all surrounding towns through their networks.

The Camp Verde Yavapai-Apache

An Act of 1 August 1914 appropriated $20,000 for purchase of lands for Indians under jurisdiction of the Camp Verde Indian School, said lands to be held in trust and subject to the General Allotment Act (38 Stat. 588, c 222).

The Yavapai-Apache Band was organized under a constitution and bylaws approved 12 February 1937. A tribal corporate charter was ratified on 11 March 1948. All individuals listed on tribal rolls as of 1934 and the 1936 supplement are enrolled as members; new members are added according to certain stipulations.

The governing body is an organization known as the Yavapai-Apache Tribal Council consisting of eight members elected by the qualified voters. The council

elects from its own membership by secret ballot a chairman and vice-chairman, and from within or without its membership a secretary, treasurer and such other officers and committees as may be deemed necessary. Council officers elected from without the council membership have no vote in the council. Members hold office for two years and elections are held annually on the second Saturday of July with four councilmen being elected each year. Regular meetings are held on the second Saturday of January, April, July, October, and December. (Kelly, Wm. H. 1953:57)

These meetings are held at the Middle Verde Indian Community, at 9:00 a.m.

The Camp Verde Reservation

Actually this reservation is comprised of two parts: one located on the outskirts of the town of Camp Verde, which consists of some forty acres of farmland, mostly undeveloped; and a second area about six miles to the northwest known as Middle Verde. The latter holding was established about 1916, when the U.S. government purchased 460 acres of land for use of the Indians. The paid price of $22,500 included water rights and interest in the irrigation canals which supply water to Indian and non-Indian farmers. This system is operated under a cooperative ditch association, and operation and maintenance costs are met by assessments against those using the water. A few acres are used for nonirrigated farming, 70-odd for irrigated farming, and more than 400 acres for grazing cattle.

Around two hundred of the Yavapai here share the reservation with perhaps two hundred and fifty Tonto—with whom it is said cooperation has always been difficult. The term "Tonto" has been applied to a number of distinct peoples of Apache and Yuman affiliation. "It is said to have been given to a mixture of Yavapai, Yuma, and Maricopa, with some Pinaleño Apache, placed on the Verde River Reservation, Arizona, in 1873, and transferred to the San Carlos Reservation in 1875; also to a body of Indians, descended mostly from Yavapai men and Pinaleño women." (Swanton 1952: 365; *See* Morris 1972:105-110)

Because of the limited resources of this reservation, only a few families could derive a living from farming. Most must earn their livelihood from off-reservation employment in and around Clarkdale and Cottonwood. They do various wagework, some engage in small scale mining, and a few lease lands for farming and grazing from the Yavapai-Apache Indian Council. More than one hundred families account for a population around 450.

Medical facilities are not provided locally for the Camp Verde Yavapai, but patients are cared for at the hospital in Cottonwood, under contract with the government.

The Yavapai Indians at Prescott

An Act of 5 June 1935 transferred seventy-five acres of land in Arizona from the Veterans' Administration to the Department of Interior, title to remain in the U.S.A. in trust for the Yavapai Indians (49 Stat. 332, c. 202). Agency headquarters is in Valentine.

This group, numbering about ninety, lives on the north edge of the city of Prescott, in an area of rolling hills on which juniper, piñon and live oak grow. Land within the reservation accommodates homesites and necessary community developments, including a cemetery. The soil is rocky and water is in short supply, so agriculture is not practiced. Adjoining acreages amounting to 500 acres are used for a small stockraising enterprise. Most of the Indians' income is derived from wagework in Prescott. This group has not adopted a constitution, but operates under an informal five-member board, which represents them in administrative matters. The board meets the second Friday of each month. Elections are held on the second Friday in July, every second year. Law and order is handled by Yavapai county and has been very effective; the expenses are met by the county and the State of Arizona.

Education for the young people of this group and for those on the Camp Verde Reservation is through the public schools. Medical facilities are provided for the Prescott Indians, under contract with the government and local physicians.

THE "PAYSON APACHE"

Recently a group of people designated as Payson Apache, numbering eighty-five and dwelling in a small community within the confines of the Tonto National Forest in Arizona, sent two of their articulate representatives to Washington, D.C., to seek trust title to 85.9 acres of land upon which they live. Above all, they sought legal recognition of the Payson Apache Indian community as a tribe—a status the federal government has long denied. (*See* Brandon 1970a:35*; 1970b:27†)

Troubles stem from gold-discovery days in the 1860's. "The Rio Verde Reserve was established in 1871 for the Tonto and Yavapai Indians. But it was dissolved four years later, and the Payson Apaches claim their Tonto ancestors were forcibly removed to the San Carlos Reservation." Then, "About the turn of the century, some of the Tontos returned to Payson and took up residence in the forest just south of town. Now, about 70 years later, these Payson Apaches are considered squatters in the eyes of the law."

As the Apache representatives in Washington pointed out, because they are not considered a tribe and live on National Forest land they have not been able to bring in electricity, running water or sewage facilities. Most of their houses are made of scrap lumber from nearby mills, or of old lumber. All of the adult males are employed in the saw and planer mills; and none of the Payson Apache families are on welfare.

Despite the fact that certain Arizona legislators have introduced legislation and given other support in behalf of these Indians,

---

*" 'Indian Community' means a tribal community with a quasi-sovereignty of its own and a sense of relatedness among its people akin to that of a religious community."

†"The people of an Indian community generally will not sell out for individual opportunities no matter how alluring; will undergo any privations to remain part of their living community. The community superlife, calling for inter-personal harmony rather than inter-personal striving, is in absolute opposition to the orthodox American gods of work-as-a-virtue and amassing personal wealth as a measure of success."

their success to date has been nil. A speaker for the Department of the Interior has remarked that title can be given to the land requested by the Payson Apache, but he says they should not now recognize them tribally. In the attitude of so many bureaucrats, an assistant secretary for Public Land Management is quoted as saying: "We do not now recognize this group and believe that we should not now recognize them. If this group wishes to avail itself of Indian services, they need only remove themselves to the San Carlos Indian Reservation, which they have refused to do for a number of reasons." (Anonymous 1971a)

Since the San Carlos reservation is some one hundred miles from Payson, as the Indians point out, "to move there would require a mass uprooting of the Payson Apaches," and "establishment as a corporation would provide them no security and would force them to pay taxes." Recognition as a tribe would allow them to be recipients of the vast array of BIA services, ranging from education to health and economic development.

SMALL AND WARM

She was small and warm
her hands like cotton
her face like ropes
her hair like a waterfall
her smile like a stone
her mind like the sky
her life like a river
her death like the fever of sorrow
her memory small and warm

By Courtney Moyah, Pima-Apache

From: *Art and Indian Children.* Curriculum Bulletin No. 7, 1970. Institute of American Indian Arts, Santa Fe, N. M.

.... THE PIMANS

BRIEF HISTORY   The Piman peoples have a long history which reaches back into the prehistoric past. First reporting of the Pima began in 1539 by Fray Marcos de Niza, the Franciscan who introduced Christianity. Jesuit missionaries encountered Piman-speaking Indians in the state of Sonora, in northwestern Mexico, and these came to be designated as the Lower Pima when, some seventy-five years later, missions were extended into present day Arizona, *Pimería Alta*, or the territory of the Upper Pima. The Upper Pima were "a single tribe" only in that they spoke a single language. Marked cultural differences existed. Those Pima dwelling in the San Pedro valley (the Sobaipuri) and on the Gila plain, for instance, "lived in fairly concentrated rancherias sustained by agriculture," while those farther west were nomadic food-gatherers. "Moreover, there was no permanent political organization linking more than a few rancherias in any part of the Pimería. Political coordination of rancherias for any purpose but warfare seems to have been unknown, although there were games and customs of ceremonial cooperation between the rancherias. The widest political organization probably did not link more than fifteen hundred people. (Spicer 1970:119)*

It has been recorded that when the early Spaniards encountered the valley dwellers of the Gila and Salt rivers, they asked many questions of them. The usual Indian reply was *pi-nyi-match*, or "I don't know." From this, the Spaniards took to calling them "Pima." The name by which they indicate themselves is *ah-kee-mult-o-o-tom*, meaning "River People." Thus the term *Pima*, like the word *Apache*, has no linguistic significance.

Father Eusebio Francisco Kino, an energetic Italian, who was as much an explorer as a missionary, came among the Pima in 1687, intent upon reducing the ranchería people to pueblo dwellers. His campaign lasted for twenty-five years, keeping, it is said, "at a high intensity conflicts of interest between the Indians and the Spanish settlers." The Pima were considered wild and difficult, extremely savage, inasmuch as they resisted impressment by the Spaniards for work in the developing Mexican mines and on the ranches.

Kino soon demonstrated that the majority of the Pima were friendly, industrious, and peaceful, ready to ally themselves with the Spaniards, or to live quietly under the mission system. Kino

*Quotations from Spicer reproduced by permission of the University of Arizona Press.

introduced livestock, wheat and other crops which the Indians readily accepted, along with metal tools. He found them carrying on some trade with other indigenous peoples, but this did not comprise an important part of their economy. By standards of the day, the Pima were better off than neighboring groups. Lacking a highly developed social organization, they did not persist in their native religious ceremonies after contact with the Spaniards and Christianity.

In the regions where the Piman peoples dwelt, little attire was necessary. Women wore a one-piece, wrap around skirt, reaching from waist to the knees. These were made of a piece of deerskin or from home-woven cotton cloth. Men wore a loincloth of the same materials, and sometimes sandals, fashioned from mountain sheep skin or of twisted fibers. The hair of all individuals was allowed to flow freely—a chief sign of beauty. Ornaments of turquois and other stones were made into ear pendants; these sometimes hung to the shoulders; they were worn by men and women alike.

Women especially painted designs on their bodies for special occasions. And they were tattooed with lines that extended from the mouth to the chin. Although a painful practice, all girls over sixteen years old had these decorations. Youngsters ran about naked most of the time.

Kino died in 1711, after which the missions soon became a thing of the past. The Pima revolted against the Spaniards in 1751, and this "constituted a shock from which the Jesuit missions had not recovered by the time of the expulsion in 1767." (Spicer 1970:132) The Franciscans who followed in missionary efforts were relatively weak, although certain individuals, such as Father Garcés, were successful in their undertakings.

On the whole, reports indicated that the Upper Pima "had returned to their 'ancient barbarism.' " And it has been said that: "An important factor in the increasing isolation was the intensification of the Apache raids after about 1810. During the late 1700's Piman-speaking people had steadily retired westward from their border position on the San Pedro River. By 1800 there were no Pimans east of a line between San Ignacio near Magdalena and San Xavier. Many had been killed, and a few had been absorbed into the central Sonoran communities of Opatas and Spaniards. The remaining Pimans, who were not at the mission sites along the Santa Cruz and Magdalena, were living in desert villages in the present area of the Papagos or the river villages along the Gila." (Spicer 1970:132-133)

In the early 1800's the Franciscans exerted themselves to bring the Pima into the Santa Cruz River missions (San Xavier and Tumacacori), and apparently were successful in getting numerous converts.

The Apache raids were intensified during the 1830's and 1840's, and the following decade saw the raiding extended throughout the southern Upper Pima domain, past the Altar valley to the coast of the Gulf of California.

Through the Gadsden Purchase in 1853, the Piman land holdings became a part of the U.S.A. This transaction brought about immediate and important changes in the lives of the Upper Pima. Foremost was the different political condition.

The new international boundary surveyed in 1858, traversed the region of the headwaters of the San Pedro and Santa Cruz rivers and ran through the middle of the desert lands to the west. This automatically placed at least three-quarters of the remaining Upper Pima as residents of the United States. As much as sixty years later there were still Pima in the dèsert rancherías, under the leadership of a headman named Pia Muchita, who seemed unaware of the change and still professed allegiance to Mexico. Nevertheless, the invading Anglo-Americans regarded the Upper Pima territory north of the new line as part of the United States and proceeded to act accordingly. (Spicer 1970:133-134)

THE CALENDAR   The Piman year begins with the rainy season, when characteristic plants and animals appear. The year is based on the moon periods, thus a lunar calendar of twelve "moons" is followed (or was into the present day). The sahuaro, or giant cactus, which ripens at the beginning of the rainy season is highly significant in the life of the Piman peoples. It was customary for a family to establish a permanent camp in the nearest sahuaro area. The figlike fruits and seeds were gathered for food in late June and July, before the rains began. The fruit, brought down by a long, pointed staff, was fermented to yield an alcoholic beverage which was drunk ceremonially—to bring rain. (Underhill 1940:48) Sahuaro harvesting, then, marked the beginning of the new year in the native calendar.

Sahuaro ribs were used on occasion in making house walls, and calendar sticks were made from them also. Some of the recent history, dating from just before the time of the Gadsden Purchase, is recorded on notched sticks—a device like computer records to remind one of events that occurred in successive years. Perhaps six feet long, a smooth, slightly flattened inner support of the giant cactus, about an inch and a half in diameter, had mnemonic symbols representing happenings recorded on the smooth side.

In some instances, dots and circles bespeak major ceremonies for the most part, although other events may be recorded. One stick has been described as follows:

> At the beginning of each year . . . a notch is cut across the stick and, at the beginning of the next year, another, an inch or two further on. Between them is placed some crude geometrical sign, such as a triangle, cross or parallel lines to indicate the outstanding event of the year. Occasionally, two events are represented. The symbols are painted with red clay, such as was used for face paint, and blue soot collected from embers of greasewood, *Covillea glutinosa*, used for tatooing [*sic.*]. (Underhill 1938a:7)

The calendar keeper invented his own symbols. The sticks appear to have been kept in various villages. They are considered as private possessions, and it was customary to break one's stick and bury it with the owner upon his death.

The Anglos, knowing little and caring less about the Piman relationships, made distinctions between the Indians who dwelt on the Gila River (whom they often called "Pimos") and those who lived in the vicinity of Tucson and westward therefrom. The Spaniards had called the desert dwellers "Papagos," and the term became general with the Anglos for all Piman-speaking peoples who lived south of the Gila residents, whom they called the "Pima."

THE PIMA (THE RIVER PEOPLE)

Living at the very northern edge of the Spanish frontier, the Pima of the Gila River valley—where they had dwelt since prehistoric times—had the least contact with the Spaniards. With permanent water from the Gila, the Pima had irrigated their agricultural lands by means of an elaborate canal system. Kino had come among them in 1694, and other missionaries followed. Spanish officials had presented canes to the Pima, as they did to the Pueblo peoples. Accepting these, or at least official designations, the Pima "had acquiesced in a nominal obedience to the King of Spain."

Friendly relations existed between the Indians and the Anglos. During the 1820's fur trappers passed through the Pima territory, following the Gila trail. On these occasions the trappers were furnished food by the Pima. Reports of these contacts and those of General Kearny and the Mormon Battalion stated that the Gila Pima were the "most civilized Indians in the United States." Thousands of Anglos traversed the Pima holdings during the gold rush to California, beginning in 1849. They, too, found the Indians friendly, peaceful, and the source of plentiful food. The Pima were anxious to trade for metal and other goods.

It was not until 1855 that Pima leaders learned that their territory had come under the control of the U.S.A. as result of the Mexican War and the Gadsden Purchase. One of them consulted with the U.S. Boundary Commission, and was "assured that the United States had friendly intentions, that the land right under the Spaniards would be fully recognized, and also that the United States government had in mind giving the Pimas agricultural implements to assist them in the valuable service they were rendering providing food for parties of travelers." (Spicer 1970:147)

In characteristically tardy manner, it took the government four years to get the implements delivered, but the promise was fulfilled and this consolidated friendly relations between the Pima and the whites. At that time, however, the federal policy began to be applied to the Pima.

The Pima Reservation

An act of 28 February 1859 "required the President to have the boundaries of the lands then occupied by the confederated bands of Pima and Maricopa Indians near Gila River, Arizona, surveyed and to have it set apart as a reservation, not exceeding 100 square miles and $10,000 was to be presented to said Indians (11 Stat. 401, c. 66 sec. 305)." (Kelly Wm. H. 1953:61) The reservation was established south of Phoenix, on the Gila and Santa Cruz rivers; and the Pima agency was located in Sacaton about forty-two miles southeast of Phoenix, in 1871. (Robinson 1954:15) The appropriation of ten thousand dollars was used in part to buy tools for the Indians' use, but the remainder had to cover "the expense of a survey of the land on the Gila River for the purpose of setting aside not more than sixty-four thousand acres as a reservation." (Spicer 1970:149) The Pima who had lived on the Gila for centuries, having descended, it is believed, from Hohokam ancestors, claimed a much larger area; and the issue remained in dispute for a decade. In 1869, the survey was increased by 81,000 acres, giving a total of 145,000 acres—still far less than the Pima claimed.

Drought and the encroachment of settlers from the east caused the Pima to appeal to the federal government for consideration of their mounting problems. Leaders went to Washington in 1873 to present their case—and learned of the power of the white officials. "It was proposed that the Pima problems could be solved by removal to Indian territory." One of the leaders, Antonio Azul, went to Oklahoma and looked over the land to which they might be assigned. He was favorably impressed, but all the other Pima were opposed to any removal from their homeland. As result of the failing water supply some twelve hundred, or more than a quarter of the Pima group, moved north on the Salt River, where they farmed among the white settlers; the remaining Pima spread along the Gila in three major areas of water seepage, where marginal farming was carried on.

As one authority has stated:

The period ... from about 1870 to about 1900 was one of increasingly intensive contact with Anglos and of numerous changes in Pima life. The surrounding of their land by Anglo settlers became an established fact. The Southern Pacific Railraod traversed their territory in 1878. Florence on their eastern margin became an important territorial town with an increasing population. By 1887 the irrigation canal constructed to take water out of the Gila River for the white settlers utilized the whole flow. No water reached any of the Pima fields downstream. Settlers were pressing to the edge of the reservation from the south in the Casa Grande area. Protests and representations had no effect except to increase by small parcels the size of the reservation. The real need, however, was for water, not land, as most government reports recognized; yet no effort whatever was made to protect the Indian water rights. The government ignored the problem, although agents in rapid succession continued to push for the Indian rights. (Spicer 1970:149)

During all this period from 1876 to 1915 no less than a dozen US executive orders increased or reduced their land or modified the boundaries. (*See* Kelly, Wm. H. 1953:61)

New Ways for the Pima   In 1881, the BIA established a boarding school in Sacaton—long after the Presbyterian Church, which was active among the Pima, had started a day school there (in 1868). A force of Indian police was initiated, and a Court of Indian Offenses set up. "An Indian Bureau farmer was brought to the reservation to give agricultural advice. At the same time that the Indian Bureau made these efforts to give some services to the Indians, activities of the Presbyterian Church were intensified." (Spicer 1970:149)

This authority tells of the work of a particular missionary-schoolteacher (Charles H. Cook) who, following a pitched battle between two Pima villages, began a vigorous missionary campaign, not only to baptize Pima people, but in an effort to reorganize their deteriorating communities. "Poverty through lack of water with which to farm and replacement of functions formerly performed by village headmen through the government agency had resulted in some degree of demoralization of the Indians." Three distinct factions had developed from water problems.

Before 1899, the missionary had baptized half of the Pima and established churches throughout the reservation.

In each community he appointed an elder, assisted by deacons, whom he held responsible for law and order and general moral standards. The elders were usually former village headmen. Gradually a transformation in village life took place, centering around the new religious organization. Annual revival meetings took the place of old ceremonies. Christian mythology and theology replaced older beliefs and the strict morality of the Presbyterians tended to reintegrate the disintegrating villages. The church affairs were almost entirely in the hands of the local Pimas, and ministers were trained to do the preaching. The Presbyterian missionary, Cook,* became the most influential force from Anglo society among the Pimas, although at the same time the Sacaton Boarding School and other boarding schools set up elsewhere by the Indian bureau were well attended by Pimas and worked together with the missionary in the transformation of Pima society. (Spicer 1970:149-150)

Worsening Economy   Economically, conditions on the reservation continued to worsen. In 1895 food rations had to be issued by the government. Individual Pima efforts did little toward solving the overall problem. And, "The Indian Bureau attempted nothing that would involve it in the matter of water rights on the Gila. It did however begin a program for solution of the water problem—the digging of wells to be served by electric pumps—in the eastern and central part of the reservation. Some fifteen wells were put into operation between 1903 and 1910." (Spicer 1970:150)

In 1914 the BIA put an allotment plan into effect, with the result that some of the Pima began coming back to the reservation to take up ten-acre plots. The consequence was wide scattering of the Indians over the reservation, "again disrupting community life."

*NOTE: Inasmuch as the influence of one particular man on the Pima people was so great, surely he should have more than passing mention. Mr. Cook, living in Chicago in 1870, heard of the spiritual need of the Pima and recognized this as his call. No church or denomination was back of him, but he left for the Southwest, taking a small organ which cost him thirty dollars. The train, then, went only to Dodge City, Kansas. From that point Cook continued on by coach and by walking; his funds were reduced to twenty-five cents by the time he reached Cow Springs, New Mexico.

Preaching along the way resulted in an unexpected but gratifying small sum of money. Cook continued on his weary route, reaching his destination, the Sacaton agency, on 23 December. In January 1871 he was hired as a teacher to the Pima Indians, at six hundred dollars per annum. On 15 January he started a little school with thirty-five youngsters whom he found well behaved and apt for learning.

During his years of service, Cook was awarded a medal by President U. S. Grant. In his old age he retired to Iowa where he died and was buried. To the last, he loved the Pima people.

The Cook Christian Training School, at Tempe, Arizona, was established in Dr. Cook's honor, and a centennial celebration was observed on 6 February 1971—with Indian dances and singing, art exhibit and a drama of Cook's life, and an open pit barbecue. In March a formal banquet was held. (*See* Walker 1970)

Climatic
Influences

Although the Gila River Indian Reservation of today encompasses 371,932 acres—good farming land, if irrigated, and nonirrigable stretches—the physical conditions influence the lives of the approximately 5,300 souls who are enrolled there. Pima comprise the majority, with a few Maricopa and Papago included in the census. At Sacaton, which may be reached by Arizona Highways 87 and 93, the highest rainfall occurs in July and August, and summer temperatures have been as high as 117°F. The lowest rainfall is in April, May and June. The temperature rarely goes below 20°. Mean daily range of temperature between day and night is 35°. The frost-free period is about 263 days.

Largely through efforts of representatives of the Presbyterian Church, the San Carlos Project Bill was passed in 1924, and construction of a dam near the old San Carlos Apache agency was initiated. This promising action was welcomed by the Pima and many began returning to their reservation to make land ready for the water. Two years later, an advisory council of Pima men was formed by the BIA, primarily to have some tribal body with which to deal on legal matters pertaining to the entire Pima group.

In 1930, after completion of Coolidge Dam and the San Carlos reservoir, preparation for the new supply of irrigation water began. "At the same time extensive road-building programs were instituted, there was a shift to day schools from boarding school, and agricultural extension service was put into operation. In 1934 under the Indian Reorganization Act the Pima prepared a constitution and formed a tribal council. In 1937 District Farmers Associations were formed over the reservation, and in 1938 a high school was established at Sacaton." (Spicer 1970:151)

The farm program resulted in misunderstandings and disputes, and loss of prestige of the tribal council. Family income declined and the Pima farmers lost interest. In 1951 the council initiated a tribal farm which became a paying venture; but individual farming declined in importance.

Assimilation

At the time, 94 per cent of all the Pima were literate, and 98 per cent spoke English. It has been said that, "The Gila Pimas probably were the most nearly culturally assimilated of all Indians in New Mexico or Arizona. The Pima Tribal Council continued in operation but it did not function as a political institution for Pimas as a whole. The tribe as a unit of social organization or culture had ceased to exist in the Arizona milieu. The tribal organization existed as a rather specialized mechanism for managing some economic matters for Pima settlements nearest the agency." (Spicer 1970:151)

Modern Government   The Gila River Pima-Maricopa Community was organized under a constitution and bylaws approved 14 May 1936, and a tribal corporate charter was ratified on 28 February 1938.

In establishing tribal status:

> All individuals listed on the official allotment roll of the Gila River Reservation are members. New members are added as follows: (1) all descendants are entitled to membership if they are of at least one-quarter degree of Indian blood—those having a lesser degree may be admitted to membership by a majority vote of the council of the community; (2) members who have remained away from the reservation continuously for a period of 20 years and automatically forfeited their membership may be reinstated by a majority vote of the council with the consent of the district in which he or she proposes to take up residence; and (3) persons of Indian blood marrying members of the Gila River Pima-Maricopa Indian Community may be adopted into the community by a three-fourths vote of the council. (Kelly, Wm. H. 1953:61)

A community council made up of seventeen members is the governing body; these must be twenty-five years of age or over, and a resident for at least one year immediately preceding the election of the district from which he or she is elected. Councilmen hold office for three years, with one-third of the membership being elected each year. The council meets on the first Wednesday of each month at 9:00 a.m., in Sacaton, Arizona. Meetings on the third Wednesday of each month are held in the districts. All tribal officers, committees, and extra law enforcement officers are selected by the council. Tribal officers are selected from within or without council membership; if selected from without the membership they do not have a vote in the council. The presiding officer, however, has the right to vote in case of a tie. (Kelly, Wm. H. 1953:62)

Affairs of the community are in the hands of fifteen committees, each with its chairman. The committees are concerned with: Arts and Crafts, Education, Farm Board, Government and Management, Health, Homesite, Housing Authority, Irrigation, Land Board, Model Cities Program, Planning and Zoning, Police Commissioners, Skill Center, Social Development, and Youth Home Board. In addition, chairmen are named for the Gila River Development, Gila River Indian Enterprises, Gila River Products Corporation, Pima-Chandler and Pima-Coolidge districts, Pima Education and Agricultural Development Corporation, and the SanTan Industrial Development Corporation.

Officers of the community are a governor, lieutenant governor, secretary, treasurer, tribal judge, and police chief. The council has jurisdiction over all matters pertaining to the management of tribal property, conduct of Indians and non-Indians on the reservation, tribal business enterprises, and the welfare of tribal members.

The tribal court at Sacaton handles

all cases within the Pima Agency jurisdiction which includes, besides the Gila River Pima-Maricopa Community, the Salt River Pima-Maricopa Community, the Fort McDowell Community, and the Maricopa (Ak-Chin) Community. The judge and associate judge are appointed by the Indian Service and their salaries are paid by the government. The clerk of the court is appointed by the Governor with the approval of the Community Council and receives his salary from court funds. The chief of police, also appointed and paid by the Indian Service, serves the Pima Agency jurisdiction. (Kelly, Wm. H. 1953:62)

Present-Day Economy

Principal income for years has come from leases of lands to white farmers. Other revenue is derived from traders' licenses, apiary rents and sand and gravel sales. Since 1 July 1966 the Gila River Indian Community has been in the midst of what is almost "a non-native revival movement, a home-grown and BIA and OEO supported economic, social, and political development program they call *Vh-thaw-hup-ea-ju*, 'It Must Happen'." (Fontana 1967) This was set up as an eighteen-month accelerated program with some fifty-one projects. By the end of the first year significant progress had been made, and has continued under the direction of the Indians but utilizing resources and assistance available from the BIA, federal and state agencies, and those of neighboring communities.

The Gila River Indian Community has attacked the problem of unemployment by luring industry to the reservation and preparing the available work force for jobs in industry. The industrial development is centered primarily in three industrial parks, the site improvement of which is being funded by the Economic Development Administration. This development was geared to be supplemented by service facilities, commercial enterprises and residential construction. Systematic development of the interchange areas on Interstate Highway 10 was also part of the program. It was anticipated that by the end of 1968 a significant number of new jobs would be created on the reservation. Other aspects of economic development centered around increasing income from agriculture and development of the reservation mineral potential. (Cumming 1967)

Social Development   The Ecomonic Opportunity Act of 1964 provided stimulus to social development on the reservation. The Community Action Program has a number of components: Headstart, Day Care Center for children, guidance, adult education, alcoholism prevention and treatment, health aides, and community improvement. Other OEO activities include a NYC program, a state-administered Title 5 work experience program, VISTA program, and agricultural loans under Title 3.

The BIA branch of Social Service, HEW (division of Indian health) social workers personnel of Title 5, and the Gila River Indian Community Action Program cooperate in social service programs aimed at helping those families with social problems to make satisfactory adjustments.

During 1967 the public school was consolidated with the BIA school at Sacaton. The facilities are used jointly, and the first grade was transferred from the BIA to the public school. Thenceforth, each year, a successively higher grade has been transferred, with the end that the BIA school will be phased out.

Since 1966 an increasing number of new, mutual self-help houses have been built. In the Casa Blanca area, many new bathrooms were added to existing structures. Several modern homes have been constructed through FHA insured loans, and a number have been renovated. Water and sanitation systems have been improved at Casa Blanca and Upper SanTan.

One of the major objectives of the Vh-thaw-hup-ea-ju plan was to improve management and government by the Gila River Indian Community. Projects included a review of the Community constitution, development of a tribal roll, codification of tribal ordinances, development of a law and order code, and a management review of the community organization structure.

As in many of the other Indian communities, the primary function of the BIA agency is coming to be one of providing services to the Gila River Indian Community and individual Indians, so that they may better attain their goals.

Pima Arts   Pima women have long been noted for their beautifully woven and artistically decorated basketry. These have enjoyed many useful purposes. Three native materials are employed: willow, devil's claw (*Martynia*), and cattail, or tule (*Typha angustifolia*). The weavers harvest these at the proper seasons, prepare them for future use, and store them away until the time comes.

In the old days it was estimated that six out of ten Pima women were basket weavers. Today the number has dwindled to a few. This art entails time-consuming labors. The late Bert Robinson has described the making of basketry by the Pima and other Indian peoples of Arizona in an extensively illustrated volume that is recommended to interested readers. (Robinson 1954)

Three types of designs are used by the Pima: geometric, symbolic, and original. The fret design is the most commonly employed. None of the designs are drawn, but are carried in the mind of the weaver, just as the designs of pottery makers. A squash blossom design is next in popularity, and is executed in numerous variations. Another attractive design is known as butterfly wings; and among the favored ones is the whirlwind—an oft occurring phenomenon of the Southwestern desert areas. Star designs are infrequently used. In some instances, design motifs may be used in combination with other features, such as swastikas and coyote tracks. Original designs are not very common.

The most universal form of Pima basketry is that of relatively shallow bowls. Formerly made in quantities, storage baskets woven of wheat straw and the bark of young mesquite trees have become increasingly rare. Basketry jars are made in various sizes, and they are almost exclusively for the tourist trade, as are miniature specimens. A few of the Pima weavers make baskets of horse-hair—again for the tourists; they are fine little items. The old type of burden basket, or *giho* (*kiaho*), has not been made for many years.

Much of their traditional ceremonialism has been lost to the Pima, yet native social urges are present. Annual fairs are favorite celebrations. On a Saturday and Sunday in March, one may witness the *Mul-chu-tha*, or fair, at Sacaton, south of Phoenix. They have a rodeo; parade and exhibits; and Indians from several of the Pima villages, such as Bapchule, assemble to present rain and basket dances, and to engage in a *taka* game and various contests. It is now customary to select a Miss Mul-chu-tha Queen annually.

THE PAPAGO (THE DESERT PEOPLE)   The native name for these Piman-speaking people, *Tóno* (TOH-ono) *oóhtam*, signifies "people of the desert." They have, among other designations, been called *papáh óotam*, or "bean people." (Swanton

1952:357) They occupy the southwest portion of the Southwest—the foothills and valley floors of northern Sonora (Mexico) and southern Arizona.

It appears that Father Kino was the first white man to visit their territory, in 1694. He found them living essentially as they did until very recent times. Other than not having so much contact with the whites as did the Pima, the history of the two groups has been similar. Cultural differences are minor. They recognize themselves as one people. The location of the Papago has made them less agricultural than the Pima; in early times some of the former completely lacked farming opportunities.

CELEBRATION

I shall dance tonight.
When the dusk comes crawling.
There will be dancing and feasting.
I shall dance with the others
    in circles,
        in leaps,
            in stomps.

Laughter and talk
    will weave into the night,
Among the fires of my people.
Games will be played
and I shall be
    a part of it.

By Alonzo Lopez, Papago
From: *The Writer's Reader*, 1962–1966, The Institute of American Indian Arts, Santa Fe, N. M.

The Papagueria   The lands of the Papago—*Papagueria*—are hot and arid. Elevation runs from 1,400 to 3,000 feet, encompassing extensive flat plains from which short mountain ranges or peaks rise rather abruptly. Rainfall varies in different parts of the area, amounting to from four to twelve inches during the year. Typically desert vegetation grows there: "creosote predominates the low dry plains, mesquite and paloverde line the usually dry stream beds, and the hill slopes are variably covered with cacti." (Gabel 1949:12)

Two periods of rain occur, one in winter and one in summer;

the latter permits limited, undependable farming. Understandably, the Papago long engaged in hunting—chiefly of rabbits, some deer, antelope, and other animals—and gathering wild foods; and they traveled considerable distances to get drinking water. Basically, and largely for these reasons, they were somewhat less sedentary than the Pima. During the summer they moved from their more permanent villages in the foothills, where the water supply was constant, to lower areas where they could take advantage of increased opportunities for farming and food gathering afforded by the rains. They were good farmers who worked their small plots intensively. Their aboriginal crops were maize, beans, pumpkins, gourds and cotton. The wild foods consisted of yucca and cactus buds and fruits, mesquite beans, seeds of ironwood and paloverde, certain greens (such as amaranth, lamb's quarter, saltbush, and *cañaigre*), and sand root—sometimes called wild potato.

No permanent streams or lakes are in the Papago territory, and springs are widely scattered, The usually dry, sandy washes, or arroyos, carry flood waters for short distances and then spread out on the flood plains. Such a place is known as *Ak Chin*, "mouth of the arroyo." Several locations were so called by the Papago. This confused the government people, with result that the designation was conferred on a single village south of the Maricopa station on the Southern Pacific Railroad, on Vecol Wash.

The generally inhospitable nature of the Papago habitat helped spare the Indians from white aggressions to a degree. Yet, following the Gadsden Purchase, when the land of Papaguería was considered available for non-Indian settlement, "many springs, wells and grazing areas were soon claimed by ranchers moving into the area. Little was done to secure land for the exclusive use of the Papagos. . . ." (Papago Indian Agency 1970:12) The nature of the region, to some extent, "made the Americanization of the Papago a relatively peaceful and unhurried process. It was not until the twentieth century that miners and cattlemen began encroaching in sufficient numbers to create the need for a reservation." (Gabel 1949:15)

Reservations Anglo Style

On 1 July 1874 an executive order established a reservation adjoining the city of Tucson, San Xavier del Bac. Next, an executive order of 12 December 1882 set apart lands just north of Gila Bend for the Papago living there; and an executive order of 16 June 1911 established small reserves of 80 acres each at Indian

Oasis (now Sells) and San Miguel. Four executive orders of 28 May 1912 set up the Maricopa, Cockleburr, *Chui Chuisch,* and *Tat-murl-ma-kutt* reservations.

Then it followed that:

An Executive Order of December 5, 1912, added another reservation at the foot of Boboquivari Peak—Santiergos. An Executive Order of January 14, 1916, established the "Sells," Nomadic Papago, or Papago Villages, Reservation which included the area formerly within the Cockleburr, Chui Chuische, Tat-Murl-Ma-Kutt, land (the Maricopa Reservation became a part of the Piman Indian Reservation). Congressional Acts in 1926, 1931, 1937, and 1940 authorized the purchase of patented land to be added to the Papago Reservations in addition to inclusion of public domain land." (Papago Indian Agency 1970:12)

All of the orders and acts brought about a total of 2,855,984 acres of reserved lands for use of the Papago Indians. Within the present Sells reservation are 2,774,370 acres; 71,201 acres within the San Xavier reservation; and 10,409 within the Gila Bend reservation. The main reservation stretches ninety miles across Pima county, and from the Mexican border north to within about ten miles of the town of Casa Grande, Arizona. Of the Papago holdings only some 7,000 acres are irrigated; about 1200 acres are at San Xavier. It is said that "Little change of any importance in Papago land holdings has been made since 1940's, but a very important change in the nature of Indian title came about in 1955 when, by Act of Congress, the Papagos were given all mineral, as well as surface rights to the reservations." (Papago Indian Agency 1970:12)

Early in 1971 a grant of $82,398 was made by the BIA for a pilot project on the Papago reservation at San Xavier. Given to the environmental research laboratory of the University of Arizona, the money was to be used for "designing and studying the feasibility of establishing controlled greenhouses on Indian reservations (using a technique which utilizes a farming-under-plastic idea—the plants being grown under huge sheets of plastic)." (Anonymous 1971g) If feasibility is proven for the raising and marketing of small vegetables, it was expected that construction could begin and actual marketing of products could start within the following year.

Late in the same year, an 800-acre farm, to be known as the San Xavier Indian Cooperative, was established through federal grants and loans of $115,000 to more than 175 landowners on the Papago Indian Reservation. For more than ninety years the Papago land has been divided among descendants from generation to generation "until no one landowner can make a living from the small, desert plots." (Anonymous 1971C) Products grown on the cooperative farm are to be "channeled into the commercial market, with emphasis on selling the products to other Papago Indians."

Currently, seventy-four settlements on the main reservation are inhabited, forty-three of them permanently. Nine of the communities are considered as major villages. Of these, Sells on Arizona Highway 86 is the largest, and it is the Papago headquarters; its population is approximately 1,000. The other major villages include *Ali Chukson, Topawa, Quijotoa, Gu Achi, Gu Vo, Pisinimo, Gu Oidak,* and *Chuichu.*

Administration   For purposes of administration the main reservation is divided into nine districts: Baboquivari, Chukut kuk, Gu Achi, Gu Vo, Hickiwan, Pisinimo, Schuk Toak, Sif Oidak, and Sells. The Gila Bend and San Xavier reservations make up two more districts, bringing the total to eleven. Each district has its own elected council and also elects two delegates to the Tribal Council. The latter meets on the first Friday of each month at 9:00 a.m., in Sells. Elections are held annually, the first Friday in February, in a building adjacent to the rodeo grounds. The tribal government has offices and an assembly hall there.

The basic political document of the Papago is the constitution and bylaws ratified by the tribal members on 12 December 1936, and approved by the Secretary of the Interior on 6 January 1937. The council has twenty-two members, men and women who are elected for two-year periods. Each district is self-governing in local matters under its elected District Council, made up of not less than five members. Should vacancies occur in the Tribal Council they are filled by the district councils. All individuals listed on the official census roll of 1936 are tribal members. Additional members include all children of resident members; and children born off the reservation may be adopted by the council if they are offspring of members and have at least one-half Indian parentage.

All tribal officers, committees, and tribal employees are selected by the council and serve for one year. The officers are: chairman, vice-chairman, secretary, treasurer, judge, and chief of police. Committees include: education, health, a housing authority, legal, mining board, an office of economic opportunity (OEO), and a rodeo board.

Law enforcement is a combined tribal-federal activity. Personnel includes a non-Indian investigator, a Papago captain of

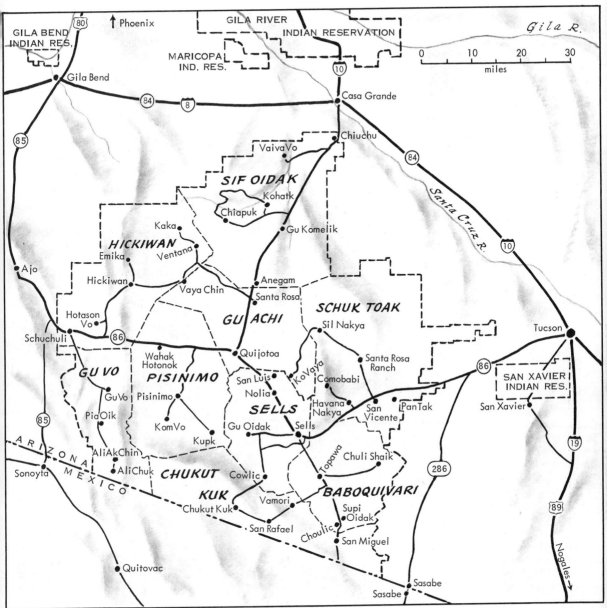

THE PAPAGO INDIAN RESERVATION, SOUTHERN ARIZONA

police, and seven tribal policemen. A radio system keeps the police department in touch with county and state police, with whom close cooperation is maintained. The first woman to hold an elective office among the Papago was selected as tribal judge. Office of the police department, jail, tribal court, and living quarters for the police captain are in the Municipal Center, a building constructed in 1962.

Economy   The Papago number about 10,000, but most of these do not live in their reservation homes all of the time; ties, however, take them back. Slightly less than 6,750 reside on the main reservation. Gila Bend residents number about 250, and San Xavier has a population of some 680. Income of the Papago has long been one of the smallest of any Indians in Arizona, but is now improving. For years, cattle raising and some subsistence farming yielded most of the livelihood. The land is overstocked and crop failures occur about one out of five years. Because of the very limited economic resources many have been forced to leave the reservation yearly to seek work of various types. A number engage in agricultural labor.

The total of Papago people employed in 1970 was 3,107. Federal employment brought in 62 per cent of all wage income. Per capita income for the Papago was then estimated to average about $700 annually.

Permanent colonies of Papago have grown up in Tucson, Casa Grande, and Ajo—south of Gila Bend on Arizona Highway 85—and in a number of other southern Arizona communities. An entirely new village has been built at Gila Bend. About forty Papago families live in the Sonoran Desert of Mexico; although they are Mexican citizens they maintain close ties with the Arizona Papago.

Dwellings   Among the changes to be observed today in Papaguería are the types of dwellings. The old Papago homes were constructed with strong, tough ocotillo (*Fouquieria splendens*) stalks or sahuaro ribs placed upright and with occasional horizontal stalks laced together and covered with adobe plaster, or wattled; sometimes, if available, rocks were used in the walls. Roofs were of ocotillo withes covered with brush.

Today, almost 65 per cent of the 980 houses enumerated on the reservation are considered to be below minimum standards. The Papago Tribal Housing Authority and the BIA are working in close cooperation with HUD to obtain modern, durable housing for the

Papago people. Present construction planning calls for five hundred new housing units by 1975.

Family Rights   In commenting on the family responsibilities of the Papago in maintenance of the household, the late Mr. Robinson said:

> If a woman needs a new dress or some article for the house, it is her responsibility to provide the money for its purchase. Likewise, the man must purchase his overalls or his harness or farm implements with *his* earnings. This attitude toward a division of communal earnings and property extends even down through inheritance rights. The parents or the brother of the husband feel that, upon his death, their right to his farm implements or livestock supersedes that of his wife, and it is only through the application of the white man's inheritance laws that justice is achieved in such cases. In the case of death of the wife, her mother or sister may make claim to personal or household articles which she had made or purchased. (Robinson 1954:42–43)

Papago Arts   Encouragement is given to the traditional art of basketry. It has been said that, despite the attention given to the making of baskets, no records have been found to indicate that they have had a part in the religious ceremonies and rituals of the Papago. They have long been highly prized, and may be kept in a family for generations. They have had extensive use as gifts; often such gifts have been buried with a recipient upon death.

No dyes are used in Papago basketry. The materials are much like those of the Pima; they are prepared and woven in natural colors. On a white (natural) background, designs are worked in green or black, or both, and occasionally in red. Thin, flexible leaves of narrowleafed yucca (*Yucca elata*) are used for white, yellow and green, and devil's claw for the black; the red is derived from yucca root or root of the desert willow (*Salix nigra*). Yucca grows only on a small portion of the Papago country. The leaves, therefore, constitute an economic item, being used by the gatherer, traded, or sold.

Papago baskets are made by the coil method with foundation bundles of beargrass (*Nolina erumpems*) or yucca, sometimes of cattail, sewn with willow splints or sotol—usually the latter if the baskets are made to be sold. Two types of stitching are used. Designs are chiefly geometric, though life forms are produced also. More devil's claw appears in the decoration of Papago baskets than in those made by the Pima. Forms include bowls—some with high curving walls, others shallow trays—jars with or without lids, tall containers with straight or outward sloping walls, miniatures, and figurines in the likeness of animals, reptiles, birds, cacti, humans, and composites of these.

The Papago produce more basketry today than any of the other Indian peoples. Nearly three thousand baskets are marketed annually through the Papago Self-help Program alone. Outstanding items are sold at many state and county fairs and rodeos, as well as in museum shops and various stores and trading posts. Outlets for basket sales have been opened in Los Angeles and Toronto, Canada; and annual sales are held in Massachusetts and New Jersey.

The use of pottery has been found to reflect "the daily life of the members of the cultures which produce it," according to a recent anthropological study. The writers of that work say:

In the case of the Papagos, canteen water jars, vessels with a small mouth and a long, constricted neck, ceased to be made when wells were drilled and when aluminum canteens were introduced. A reduction in the number of saguaro-wine vessels suggests a similar reduction in the frequency of certain Papago ceremonies. Items such as pottery ashtrays, toothpick holders, and piggy banks being made today tell us that Papago life has changed sharply in the last sixty or seventy years; these items even offer some suggestion as to the nature of this change. (Fontana et al. 1962)*

The work mentions that pottery is the keystone of much archaeological analysis, and it points out that the study of pottery of a living culture has a great deal to offer the archaeologist, "suggesting to him the culturally significant limits of pottery analysis. There is a point in the study of pottery remains which arrives at technological sherd-splitting, going beyond limits that have any meaning for the understanding of a culture. The study of Papago pottery shows at what point this is true and why it is so."

It was found in the study conducted that numerous problems relate specifically to the Papago Indians, their culture and their history, which could be clarified by examination of their pottery, modern and archaeological. "One of the most intriguing of these problems," the writers found, "is the relation between the Papago Indians and the prehistoric Hohokam culture of the same area." (Both made their ceramics by the paddle and anvil technique.)

Pottery forms and decorations, when considered as a whole, have meaning. "Both are tradition-bound, just as is the technique of making pottery. The clay body, inasmuch as the component clay and temper derive from the same environment, has meaning. So does slip. But the difficulty in always being able to distinguish Pima from Papago pottery, even at this contemporary date, should tell the student of prehistory to beware." (Fontana et al. 1962:136)

Today, the only vessels made for Indian use are bean pots, water-cooling jars, and an occasional small syrup jar. The others are made for the tourist trade—but that market is collapsing; the Papago black-on-red pottery is in little demand. It is predicted that within another generation no more Papago pottery will be manufactured. (Fontana et al. 1962:137)

Industries   The Papago tribe maintains a small herd of registered cattle under professional management; and it has the only all-Indian Credit Union in the U.S.A.

Due to an unusually severe drought, which began in 1969 and continued for several years, wells ran dry and the water holes (*charcos*), upon which the Papago cattlemen depended for water for their stock, dried up completely. Hundreds of their cattle died, reducing the already destitute people almost to total devastation. Entirely on their own, a Livestock Relief Operation was formed by the Papago. It was headed by the late Tom Segundo, a Papago graduated from the University of Chicago Law School.* The Operation determined the specific needs of the stockmen, itemized them carefully and applied to the BIA for a grant of $500,000. Reporting on this a syndicated writer stated:

A bureaucratic powwow in Washington decided to grant the Papago $200,000 of which $40,000 was to be used for overtime payments to Indian Affairs Bureaucrats. Not a single Indian was invited to the meeting.

The Washington sages also solemnly forbade the Papago to use the money for cattle feed, despite the fact this was the most urgent need. Cattle feed, it was decided in Washington, was the responsibility of tribal families. (Anderson 1969)

The same writer commented that the Papago are a proud and intelligent people; and he mentioned their domestic water supply:

Most villages have one well for a water supply. The residents have to haul water to their homes in large metal oil drums. In some cases, it has to be carried over long distances, which requires a truck. For this, the family has to pay $1 a barrel. The Indian Affairs Bureau long ago decided that plumbing was too expensive to install. (Anderson, 1969)

*Most unfortunately, Mr. Segundo, then tribal chairman, was killed at the age of fifty-one years in an air crash at Casa Grande on 6 May 1971.

With $145,000 of the BIA grant, the salaries were paid, and the Papago were enabled to buy hay and pay for water hauling, and other items. Disaster was averted. Domestic water is being supplied by the PHS.

In 1971 the Papago received more emergency funds, which provided for technical advice, mechanical equipment, and about $92,000 for buying hay and getting water relief—including cleaning of the charcos. Some of the wells are still pumping; water is hauled in critical areas. As a result, death losses have been lessened, though hot weather heightens the risk. The relations between the Papago and the BIA have been greatly improved. (Whitfield 1971)

The Past vs. the Present   Taxes on cattle sales, income from land and mineral leases, license fees paid by traders and hunters, and court fines have been the chief sources of tribal income. At the present, the Tribal Council is actively working to bring about the optimum economic development of the reservations. As a result, a new day is dawning in Papaguería, as shown by the following developments:

Two large mining companies, Hecla and Newmont, have each discovered significant deposits of high grade copper ore in the northern part of the Reservation and are now preparing for full mining operations there. Training of Papagos for this kind of employment has begun and several hundred individuals will eventually be hired as regular full-time workers receiving full-scale wages. A third mining company—American Smelting & Refining—will soon begin copper mining operations at San Xavier near Tucson.

More jobs and land lease income have been generated by the opening of the San Xavier Industrial Park in 1970; this project is coming along well. Funded by a loan-grant from the Economic Development Administration, the 40-acre park is expected to quickly attract several light industries to the San Xavier Reservation. Additional industrial acreage will be developed at San Xavier to match demand.

A planned earth dam and reservoir, to be built by the Corps of Engineers, has been approved. The project will provide run-off control and a means to irrigate many thousands of acres in the north section of the main reservation. Campgrounds, fishing, and a recreational park are being planned in conjunction with this water project. (Papago Indian Agency 1970:5)

The Papago derive between $250,000 and $300,000 per year from fire-fighting engagements. This provides employment for some 365 men.

Educational Facilities   Public educational facilities are provided on the Papago reservation by the Sells Consolidated School (Indian Oasis School District

Number 40), a Pima county grade school. Elementary schooling is provided by the federal government for those students who live an excessive distance from Sells; this is at day schools in three isolated villages and a boarding-day school at *Achi*, or Santa Rosa village. Three reservation parochial schools are maintained by the Franciscan Order.

High School education is available at federally operated Indian schools, and the Phoenix Indian School is the primary choice of the Papago students. Some attend public high schools in Tucson or go to Catholic Indian high schools, such as Saint John's at Laveen, Arizona. A few students have gone on for training at the Institute of American Indian Arts in Santa Fe, New Mexico; others are attending college. Adult education classes are conducted in several of the Papago villages through the cooperative efforts of the tribal government, the OEO, and the BIA. The Papago are diligently working toward providing adequate scholarship funds for their young people.

When Kitt Peak on the Papago reservation was selected as site for a new astronomical observatory, which was built by the National Science Foundation, the Indians were very pleased. Steller telescopes of 16, 36 and 80 inches were installed, and a giant solarscope—the largest in the world—is the only one of its particular type of construction. A wide, paved highway leads to the summit of the peak, where a large picnic area has been provided near the top. Kitt Peak is open to the public every day, from 10:00 a.m. to 4:00 p.m. The observatory is one of the most important in the country.

Other Community Facilities   The BIA and PHS offices are in Sells. For the latter, a hospital facility with a 50-bed installation, costing $2,260,000 was opened in 1961; it is entirely modern and well equipped and staffed. A Post Office building was dedicated in 1964.

Religious Groups   Religious activities are available through Catholic and Protestant groups. More than three-fourths of the Papago are of Catholic faith and have churches in every sizable village. Among the Protestants, the Presbyterian, Baptist, Assembly of God, and Nazarene denominations likewise have churches.

Festive Occasions   Today, the Papago sponsor a rodeo and fair at Sells, which is one of the most exciting shows of its kind in Arizona; it is held on the last Saturday and Sunday in October. Hardriding, working Indian cowboys display their skills in daring events. Also featured are dances and ceremonials. The Papago have erected comfortable and adequate grandstands for spectators, and they treat their guests to a barbecue.

YONDER STANDS A YOUTH

Yonder stands a youth beyond
    the fires of the sunset.
In his eyes a misty cloud floats,
    telling that he weeps.
His crystal-white tears add to
    the sea of negligence
Which stretches endlessly before him,
Barring his crossing into the
    land of happiness.
Within the palms of his hands,
He cradles the jewel of his life,
Waiting hopefully for one to
    cast it to.
But, walking the sands
    of their own contentment,
Those who have reached the shore
    refuse to look toward him.

Look yonder!
There stands a helpless youth,
    crying as a child;
Toward you,
    outstretched, his hand.

By Alonzo Lopez, Papago

From: *The Writers' Reader,* Fall, 1966. Institute of American Indian Arts, Santa Fe, N. M.

THE MARICOPA —
.... MOVERS BY CHOICE

From prehistoric times, various Yuma-speaking Indians moved up the Gila River and settled.

About the beginning of the nineteenth century a group of Yuma-speaking Indians who called themselves *Pipatsje*, or "The People," occupied an area along the Colorado River, south of present day Parker, Arizona. The Anglos called these people "Maricopas." Apparently these disagreed with the other Yuma Indians with regard to selection of their leaders. As a consequence, they withdrew from the Colorado and moved eastward up the Gila River, where they made friends with the Pima Indians. There they were given land and protection from their hostile kinsmen. The Pima and Maricopa fought as allies in the battle of 1857 against Yuma and Mohave forces, whom they defeated severely. Although the Pima and Maricopa could not understand each other's mother tongue, this proved no barrier to a lasting relationship.

The retreat of the Maricopa from the Colorado left a large area of river bottom land vacant, and it was into this territory that the Mohave expanded from the north, and the Ute-related Chemehuevi also ... to become residents of what came to be named the Colorado River Reservation.

Descendants of the Maricopa are found today among the Pima on the Gila River Reservation and on the Salt River Reservation, as previously discussed. Today, two Maricopa Indian settlements are recognized: one on the northwest corner of the Gila River Reservation and the other in the Lehi district of the Salt River Reservation. From their long association with the Pima, the Maricopa seem to have lost all knowledge of their ancestors having lived elsewhere. However, until recently they followed certain practices of the past, and it was said:

Their lives are dream directed as are the Mohaves; they cremate their dead; they have a clan-name system; and they speak the Yuman tongue .... In 1858, the U.S. Army census listed 518 Maricopas. Today, through intermarriage with Pimas they have lost most of their Yuman identity. They have adopted much of the Piman culture and are now almost one with them. (Johnston 1970:58)*

*Reproduced by permission of the University of Arizona Press.

MARICOPA ARTS   The Maricopa women produced pottery of utilitarian type, with vessels for many uses, and chiefly without design—made much like that of the Pima and Papago Indians. An outstanding ceramist of the Maricopa was Ida Redbird, whose mother, *Kwehadk*, taught her the art. Like so many of the Indian people, Mrs. Redbird had a wide command of the English language as well as her mother tongue. She served as informant and interpreter for several well known scientists. Although her eyes dimmed with advancing age, she continued to make fine pottery and contributed to the advancement of her people until the time of her tragic death. During a thunder-storm on 10 August 1971, a tree fell on her while she was resting and she was crushed to death. Her age was said to be seventy-nine. (Anonymous 1971e:21; Anonymous 1971f:1) Several other Maricopa women produce good vessels.

Their effigy pottery is traditional and is still made. But the majority of pieces decorated with black-on-red or black-on-buff are largely non-Indian in original concept; they are made for the tourist trade, and are highly popular. A variety of jars and bowls of glossy red or buff, or a combination of the two, with simple designs are attractive. The long-necked jars are adapted from an old form used for syrup, or for safe-keeping of the scalps of enemies. The Maricopa have not been producers of basketry.

Old ceremonies, the great emphasis on dreams, and distinctive native social customs now are nonexistent.

FARMING   The economy today rests mainly on subsistence farming, cotton raising, and wage work. Most of the individual Maricopa land allotments are too small to be farmed profitably; for this reason most lands are leased to non-Indians for agricultural development.

It has been noted that the Maricopa dwell on the Gila and the Salt reservations. They do not, as one might expect, live on the Maricopa Indian Reservation (Ak Chin) just south of Maricopa, Arizona. This is another good example of the confusion concerning Indian groups that has come to obtain—particularly in Arizona—since the coming of the white man. It is the Papago Indians who occupy the Maricopa Indian Reservation lands.

.... THE CAHITANS

THE YAQUI
INDIANS

Of the Indians speaking Cahitan, those known as the Yaqui (YAH-key) are the southernmost of the Indians discussed, to the South of the Papago. The Cahitan-speaking people of the UTO-AZTECAN stock lived in southern Sonora, Mexico. (*See* Kurath and Spicer 1947:11) They dwelt at the mouths of large rivers, and along the entire length of the Río Yaqui. With abundant water, they tended to have somewhat concentrated settlements, or rancherias, and practiced dry farming. The density of their population led to development of genuine tribal organization with permanent ceremonial groups. In addition to shamanism, at least rudimentary forms of priesthood came into being. Emphasis on warfare led to integratio of all the Yaqui rancherias.

Brief History

The armed intrusion of the Spaniards into the Yaqui territory was resisted from the beginning. The first contact occurred in 1533, and the Yaqui were eminently successful in the encounters. They were strong enough to set their own terms for the entrance of the Jesuit missionaries. In time, the relationship became both hostile and friendly. After a major affray in 1609, in which the Yaqui were victorious, it is said that:

> Suddenly, to the surprise of the Spaniards, the Yaquis asked for peace. This was an event which the Spanish in their chronicles spoke of as unprecedented in military history. The reasons for the Yaqui action remain uncertain; there were two versions current. One held that Hurdaide [Spanish captain head-quartered on the site of modern Sinaloa] circulated stories about the arrival of the reinforcements by sea. Another version was that the Yaquis were so impressed by the Spanish military ability and Hurdaide's miraculous escape [from the conflict] that they thought it would be safest to ally themselves with the Spaniards rather than keep on fighting. (Spicer 1970:47)

Yaqui acceptance of the Jesuit missions was rapid. For several score years unusual tranquility prevailed, with economic and religious development. Government of the towns, except for the Spanish captain-general, was in the hands of the Indians.

With the discovery of rich silver mines at Alamos in 1684, things began to change, but the Yaqui initially were not much affected. In less than a half-century, however, the antagonism of one of the Spanish governors against the missionary program led to increasing discontent. In 1740, the Yaqui and their kindred, the Mayo, revolted. Just what precipitated the revolt and what actually occurred is not known, but it was costly to the Indians and Spaniards alike. Over one thousand Spaniards were killed and more than five thousand Indians.

Practically all of the mines were abandoned; all missionaries were forced to leave; livestock was killed or driven away; and an atmosphere of suspicion and distrust had been created. (*See* Spicer 1970:52) A new governor was named and he began to rule "with an iron hand."

The Jesuits returned to the missions when things quieted down, and the governor instituted "a series of restrictive measures, requiring that no Indian be permitted to leave any pueblo without the permission of missionaries, impressing Indians for forced labor on mines and haciendas, and requiring that there be daily recitation of prayers by all Indians in the mission communities. . . . After 120 years the typical Spanish frontier situation had finally developed in the Yaqui-Mayo country. . . ." (Spicer 1970:52–53)

With the return of the missionaries to their missions—which had not been destroyed—an attempt was made to reestablish things as they had been before. But the attitude of the Indians was changed, and their old level of prosperity was not regained. The Yaqui population, like that of the Mayo, declined; it was estimated that some 23,000 Yaqui remained. This was partly due to the migrations that were taking place. It was reported in 1760 that thousands of Yaqui were living away from the lower Yaqui River settlements; the people were widely dispersed. "This emigration dismayed the missionaries and gave the civil authorities the feeling that an era of decline had set in in the formerly thriving Sonoran missions." (Spicer 1970:53) They intensified their efforts among the Indians that remained, and the civil authorities concerned themselves with ways and means of increasing economic activity.

By the early 1800's, it is said, "The blending of Spanish-Catholic theocracy and Indian democracy resulted in very stable and tightly organized communities. These communities were not, however, conceived by the Indians as units in a European nation. Rather the Yaquis and Mayos, for example, still conceived themselves as independent tribal units holding their land from immemorial times and not by fiat of the Spaniards. It was growing clear that the Spaniards were fearful of challenging that view." (Spicer 1970:59–60) It was not until the Mexican government attempted to integrate the Mayo and the Yaqui into the dominant cultural pattern that hostilities really came to a head.

After the War of Independence (1821), the Mexicans considered the Indians to be citizens of Mexico and therefore taxable. The Yaqui, who had never been taxed, consistently resisted efforts to divide their land for individual ownership; they endeavored to maintain their own local government as distinct as possible from provincial or state governments, and refused to pay taxes. Conflicts ensued. Laws were enacted to integrate the Indians. These the Yaqui could not comprehend.

Through the years administrations changed; sometimes the Indians were deeply involved, again they were left practically alone for years. Perhaps one Yaqui group would take a certain action, while another had no part in the transactions or encounters. Military conflicts were many; sometimes the Yaqui winning, and at other times their opponents. Many of the defeated Yaqui were in desperate circumstances, without food and clothing, and decimated by smallpox and other illnesses. Prisoners were sent out of the Yaqui country to work, or sold as slaves.

Beginning in the 1880's, some of the Yaqui left their homeland and moved northward into southern Arizona and settled in rancherias. They were accepted there as refugees. Of the stronger groups, some Yaqui retaliated by raiding the ever encroaching farms and ranches of the Mexicans and settlers from the U.S.A. By 1900 their numbers equaled those of the Yaqui in the old Yaqui territory. In 1919 only three of the original Yaqui towns remained. After 1900 a conspicuously large influx of Yaqui into Arizona occurred.

A visit of President Obregón to the Yaqui country in 1926 precipitated a battle between the Mexican troops and the Yaqui. As a result, more of the Indians fled to the U.S.A. to live in a half-dozen communities that had grown up in southern Arizona.

The history of the main Yaqui groups in their encounters with and reactions to the foreigners who invaded their country makes fascinating reading. The publications of Spicer, who has studied the Yaqui in great detail, and the references to other authorities which he has cited, are recommended (*see* bibliography).

The Arizona Yaqui   Our interest lies with those Yaqui who have come to dwell in Arizona. Their migrations, incidentally, have continued slowly to the present time. Here, in several recognized settlements and lesser clusters, Yaqui ceremonial organizations have persisted, minus the accompanying political organizations that affect the Sonoran Yaqui. Cultural ties are maintained between the Arizona and the Mexican groups.

Probably the best known of the Yaqui villages was Pascua, once on the outskirts of Tucson, then engulfed by the spreading metropolis, and finally demolished by an Urban Renewal project. Dwellings in Pascua were fashioned of adobe bricks and corrugated sheet iron. Each house had a yard enclosed by a wire fence, with a few trees, small plots of green and colorful flowers. Almost every family had an open ramada in which much of the living took place, and which served as a gathering center at fiestatime. At one end of the village plaza was a small church, brilliantly white; at the opposite end, the fiesta ramada which was under the direction of the ceremonial societies. A wooden cross stood in front of each of these structures. At the side was a community kitchen in which the Yaqui women prepared foods over open fires—tortillas, stew, and coffee, primarily—during the fiestas. Many ceremonies took place in the plaza. Similar scenes may be witnessed in other Yaqui villages.

Just north of the San Xavier Indian Reservation of the Papago, the Yaqui have built a whole new village, on a section of land provided by the government. At first, as they became able to do so, those who wished to leave the old village and build homes in the new community might do so. Then, with the razing of Pascua, those who had remained there moved to the new village or elsewhere. Another Yaqui settlement, Barrio Libre, has been established in South Tucson.

Other Yaqui villages are Guadalupe near Tempe, and another in the Phoenix area—Water Users Village at Scottsdale; about 1,800 Yaqui dwell in the two communities. Marana and Eloy each have Yaqui villages. All together, the Yaqui in Arizona now number in excess of 3,000. The village organization is entirely in terms of the ceremonial groups in each instance. In each of their locations the Yaqui merge with the neighboring populations, Indian and Anglo.

Having no reservation, the men have made a place for themselves in the cotton fields, on ranches and farms, in the construction trades, and in other jobs. Because the Yaqui speak a tongue foreign to the other Indians living in Arizona and the Anglos alike, and since many of them have lacked educational opportunities, the Yaqui have found these factors something of a barrier to significant economic advancement.

Yaqui Ceremonials

Being of Old Mexican origin and long influenced by the Catholic religion, the ceremonial pattern of the Yaqui is a rich blend of aboriginal and introduced traditions. The ceremonies—based on Miracle Plays of the Jesuits, in which the life of Jesus was dramatized, and to which the Yaqui added their own beliefs and rituals—are enacted with a devoted consecration. The Yaqui remember no native supernatural beings, "but legend and memory remind them of the belief, similar to that of other Indians in the Southwest, that special power was obtainable from the natural world of forests, mountains, caves, and from dreams." (Painter and Sayles 1962:5)*

The symbolism that the blood of Jesus "as it fell from the cross was by a miracle of heaven transformed into flowers," is found throughout the Yaqui ceremonies. Flowers are offered as tribute to the holy ones. Especially during Holy Week and climaxing with Easter, crowds gather in the Yaqui villages, particularly in the Tucson locations and at Guadalupe, where religious rituals, processions, dancing and pantomime continue through the night—deer dances, *matachines, pascolas, fariscos*, and related activites. At dawn special prayers greet the morning. Members of the ceremonial societies serve in "fulfillment of vows made to Jesus or to Mary in return for help in time of crisis. The work of carrying out these sacred duties is known as 'flower.' It must be done faithfully and 'with good heart' to merit heavenly reward of 'flower.' Some of the regalia is also called 'flower'." (Painter and Sayles 1962:5; *see* Spicer et al. 1971)

One who has viewed many of the colorful Yaqui cermonies and written of them, tells us that:

Melodious bells and the rustle of cocoon ankle rattles herald the arrival of the Pascolas. When a Pascola dances to the high notes of the flute and the pervasive rhythm of a drum played by one man he wears his painted wooden mask over his face and beats on his palm with a small instrument [*matraca*] that jangles like a tambourine. For the alternate music of violin and harp he pushes his mask to one side. The string that ties his hair in a top knot is called 'flower.' In addition to dancing, the Pascolas delight the people with nonsense, double talk, jokes, and stories, some of age-old tradition. (Painter and Sayles 1962)

As to a deer dance, it is said that:

With a brisk shake of his gourds and his belt of deer-hoof rattles, the Deer

*Quotations from Painter and Sayles reproduced by permission of the University of Arizona Press.

dancer makes his entrance. His headdress is a stuffed deer head tipped with red ribbons which symbolize flowers. A red ribbon between the antlers is tied in the form of a cross. The deer songs to which he dances are treasured poetry from the past, reminiscent of the forest home of the deer, of flowers, clouds, rain, and wild creatures. The three Deer singers play native instruments of water drum and swift-moving raspers. The songs and dances were originally hunting rituals. (Painter and Sayles 1962:6; *see* Spicer et al. 1971)

Visitors to the Yaqui ceremonies will better understand what they are observing if the work cited, or other sources, are read in advance. Painter and Sayles include a calendar of annual events.

It should be remarked that not only do the Yaqui of Arizona attend the ceremonies given there, but they go by the hundreds to Magdalena, Sonora, which is fifty-five miles south of Nogales, to attend the fiesta of Saint Francis of Assisi on 4 October of each year. There they mingle with the Sonoran Yaqui and Mayo, as well as with Papago and Pima peoples.

STAR, STAR, MY LITTLE ONE

Star, Star, my little one
Star, I love you.
The name Star was taken
Out of the sky
And given to you, my little one.
Let me water you with
Shining praise, listen to
Your grandmother. She shall
Give you part of her knowledge
And me, I only have love
For you.
            You will learn lots.
You will be of beauty
With the knowledge, love, courage
Following you, taking every
Step with you.
Star shine bright for
Everyone to respect
You and your name.

By Sharlene Enos, Pima

From: *Art and Indian Children.* Curriculum Bulletin No. 7, 1970. Institute of American Indian Arts, Santa Fe, N. M.

CALENDAR OF ANNUAL
INDIAN EVENTS

....

NOTE: Do NOT take pictures, make sketches or recordings, or
       take notes without obtaining permission. This is
       VERY IMPORTANT!

In the pueblos are plazas, and the ranchería peoples and other
Indian groups have their dance places, where ceremonial events are
presented. Many observances occur over a period of several days,
but of these the major portions are held in the kivas or in places
where only the initiated ones may witness them. Parts that may be
seen by the public are customarily attended by adults and children,
Indian and non-Indian.

   Remember that these are sacred and commemorative rituals. It
is expected that visitors will be *quiet and respectful.*

   Ceremonies are held in Hopiland throughout the year. The
dates of these are determined according to Hopi customs and
traditions, without reference to the BIA personnel. Exact dates are
made known a few days in advance only, even to the Hopi. During
the summertime, one or more ceremonies or dances are held usually
each weekend.

   Indian dances and ceremonies are based on Indian needs and
Indian time. To translate these to the white man's calendar is not
always practicable. It is advisable to check locally whenever
possible.

JAN 1 Taos turtle dance usually (*See* Dutton 1972a: 3-12); dances in many of the
          pueblos on New Year's and/or three succeeding days, e.g. cloud dance at San
          Juan.

JAN 3 Isleta corn, turtle, and various dances

JAN 6 King's Day: installation of secular officers; dances in most of the pueblos
          during afternoon; buffalo or deer dance at Taos, eagle dance at San Ildefonso.
          Dancing in the Keres pueblos. Dancers go to the houses of people named *Reyes*
          (kings), where dwellers are waiting on the roofs. After the dancers perform for
          a while, the house owner and family members throw gifts to the dancers below
          and the gathered crowd. Everybody scrambles for presents, but most are aimed
          directly to the dancers. The gifts include bread, canned and boxed foods, fruit,
          tobacco, soft drinks, and household items. Many pueblos have dances on the
          three succeeding days.

103

JAN 23   San Ildefonso feast day—animal dances in one plaza, Comanche dance in the other

JAN   (Late January) Acoma and Laguna governor's fiesta

FEB 2   San Felipe buffalo dance; also dances in several other pueblos

FEB 4–5   *Llano* dances, *Los Comanches,* at Taos (Spanish-American interpretation of Plains Indian dances)

FEB 15   Dances at San Juan; perhaps turtle dance at Taos, eagle dance at Santo Domingo

FEB   (Usually in February) Hopi *Powamú* (bean dance)—first rites of the katsina cult

FEB   (Late February) Isleta evergreen dance

MAR   (Palm Sunday) Most pueblos, green corn dances, ceremonial foot races

MAR-APR   (Easter Sunday and succeeding two or three days) Dances in most pueblos; ceremonial foot races. Several pueblos observe ditch-opening, or *acequia,* ceremonies with dances; some play ceremonial shinny.

MAR-APR   (During Holy Week, with the climax on Easter) Yaqui Indians have elaborate celebrations at Barrio Libra (south Tucson) and at Guadalupe near Phoenix. Deer dancers, *matachines, pascolas, fariseos,* et al., take part. (*See* Painter and Sayles 1962:24) On the first Friday after Easter, the Tucson Festival Society sponsors an annual pageant that commemorates the founding of Mission San Xavier del Bac. Papago and Yaqui dancers participate.

MAR   Phoenix Plains Indian Club sponsors Scottsdale All-Indian Day

MAR   Gila River Pima *Mul-chu-tha* at Sacaton, Arizona

MAR 27   Dances generally at the Keres pueblos and Jémez

MAR   (Late March) Indian Trade Fair, Pima-Maricopa and Yavapai-Apache communities, near Scottsdale, Arizona

SPRINGTIME   Colorado River tribes hold motor boat races and Northern Yuma County Fair at Parker, Arizona

APR   (Last Saturday) *Nizhoni* dances at Johnson Gymnasium, University of New Mexico, Albuquerque; numerous Indian groups in beautiful costumes (benefit)

APR or MAY   Ute Mountain Ute bear dances

MAY 1   San Felipe feast day, green corn dance (two large groups)

MAY 3   Taos ceremonial races (about 8:00-10:00 a.m.); Cochiti corn dance (Coming of the Rivermen)

MAY 14   Taos San Ysidro fiesta (blessing of fields); candle light procession May 15

MAY   (About 29 May through June 4) Tesuque corn or flag dance (blessing of fields)

MAY   (Late May) Salt River Pima Industrial Fair

MAY   (Last week of May or first week of June) Southern Ute bear dance

JUNE 6   Zuñi rain dance

JUNE 13   Sandía feast day, corn dance; observance of San Antonio's Day dances at Taos (corn dance), San Juan, Santa Clara, San Ildefonso, Cochiti, and Paguate

JUNE 20   Isleta governor's dance

JUNE 24   San Juan feast day, dancing there; observance of San Juan's Day dances at Taos (afternoon), Isleta,* Cochiti, Santa Ana, Laguna; Acoma and Jémez rooster pulls

JUNE 29   San Pedro's Day at Laguna, Acoma, Santa Ana, San Felipe, Santo Domingo, Cochiti, and Isleta—generally rooster pulls

JUNE   (Late June, or during July) Hopi *Nimán* ("going home")—last rites of the katsina cult; katsinas are believed to go to their traditional home on San Francisco Peak. One of the ceremonial officers from Shungopavi announced that the Nimán rites and snake dances are closed because "rules against recording, picture taking and hand-drawing have been disregarded again by both Hopis and non-Indians . . . and sacred prayer feathers have been taken away." (Action Line, *Albuquerque Journal,* 15 August 1972)

JULY 1-4   Mescalero Apache *Gáhan* ceremonial at Mescalero, New Mexico

JULY 4   Jicarilla Apache feast (no ceremonies); Nambé celebration at Nambé Falls—special events and dances

JULY 4   Flagstaff Pow-Wow (Check annually)

JULY 14   Cochiti, feast day of San Buenaventura—corn dance

JULY   (Mid-July or August) Ute sun dance, Ignacio, Colorado

JULY 24   Acoma rooster pull

JULY 25   Santiago's feast day at Acoma, Laguna, Cochiti, and Taos—dances, rabbit hunt

JULY 26   Feast day of Santa Ana, corn dances; also at Taos

JULY   (Late July) Santa Clara festival at Puyé cliff ruins; arts and crafts exhibits, dances (entrance fee entitles one to take photographs)

AUG 2   Jémez, old Pecos bull dance

AUG 4   Santo Domingo feast day, corn dance—large and fine; two groups

AUG 10   San Lorenzo's feast day; corn dances at Picurís, Laguna, and Acomita

AUG 12   Santa Clara feast day; corn dances

AUG 15   Zía feast day of Nuestra Señora de la Ascensión; dances

AUG   (Two weeks before Labor Day) Dances in patio of Palace of the Governors in Santa Fe, in conjunction with annual Indian Market sponsored by the Southwestern Association on Indian Affairs

AUG 28   San Agustín fiesta at Isleta

AUG   (Late August) Hopi snake dance—a solar observance; in even years at

---

*Since Isleta adopted its constitution, the ceremonial calendar has undergone various changes. One may see dances performed by either the Laguna group which dwells in the pueblo, or by the Isleta group. Dates should be checked annually.

Shipaulovi, Shungopavi, and Hotevila; in odd years at Mishongnovi and Walpi. Usually takes place about 4:00 p.m. Alternately, when snake dances are not held in a village, flute ceremonials are given. The dances are announced sixteen days before they are due to happen.

See note under June (late) or during July.

SEPT 1	Southern Ute fair
SEPT 2	Acoma feast day of San Estéban—corn dance atop mesa
SEPT 4	Isleta feast day, harvest dance
SEPT 8	Encinal (Laguna) harvest and social dances
SEPT 8	San Ildefonso, harvest dance*
SEPT 14-15	Jicarilla Apache celebration at Horse or Stone Lake
SEPT	(Mid-September, or earlier) Navajo Tribal Fair, Window Rock, Arizona—exhibits, horse races, rodeo, dances
SEPT 19	Laguna, feast day of San José; harvest dance and others; trading
SEPT 29	Taos, sundown dance—begins at sunset
SEPT 30	Taos, feast day of San Gerónimo—relay races (early) and pole climbing; dancing
SEPT	(Usually in September) Hopi *Maraüm*, women's social function
FALL	(Some time in fall) Fall Southern Ute Fair; rodeo; Northern Ute sundance
OCT	(1st week) Annual Navajo Fair at Shiprock, New Mexico
OCT 4	Nambé, feast day of San Francisco (Saint Francis); dancing
	At Magdalena, Sonora, Mexico, the Fiesta of Saint Francis of Assisi; hundreds of Papago, Pima, Yaqui, and Mayo Indians (who are affiliated with the Yaqui) converge there each year.
OCT	(Last Saturday and Sunday) Papago rodeo and fair at Sells, Arizona
OCT 31-NOV 2	On one of these days, ceremonies in most of the pueblos; gifts to the padres, and gifts to the dead placed on graves
OCT	(Usually in October) Hopi *Oáqol,* women's social function
NOV 1-2	In the San Xavier cemetery, near Tucson, hundreds of candles are lighted around the graves at night; this is true in all Papago cemeteries
NOV 12	Jémez and Tesuque, feast day of San Diego; dances
NOV	(Usually in November) Hopi *Wüwüchim*—tribal initiation ritual for all boys about 10-12 years

---

*Because so many San Ildefonso Indians work at Los Alamos, the ceremonies traditionally held at this time of the year have been shifted to the weekend closest to the old dates. The same situation prevails at San Juan, Santa Clara, and Tesuque with regard to dances. Check dates annually.

NOV   Colorado River tribes two-day rodeo at Parker, Arizona

NOV-DEC   (Some time in November or December) The *Shalako* at Zuñi; dancing in new houses and in house of the Koyemshi

Navaho reservation Nightway and Mountain Topway ceremonies

DEC 3   Ceremony at San Xavier in honor of Saint Francis Xavier

DEC 10-12   Fiesta of Tortuga Indians in honor of Our Lady of Guadalupe, near Las Cruces, New Mexico: processions and dancing

DEC 12   Guadalupe day at Isleta and Santo Domingo—gift throwing

DEC 12   Jémez *matachines;* Tesuque flag, deer, or buffalo dances

DEC 25   Taos deer or *matachines* dance (afternoon)

Christmas Day and two or three days following, dances at most of the pueblos

DEC 31   *New Year's Eve,* before midnight mass and dancing in church at Laguna, Sandía, San Felipe, Santo Domingo, and other pueblos

DEC   In the various Hopi villages, *Soyala*—winter solstice rites; opening of the katsina season, the purpose of which is to induce the sun to start on the first half of its journey. After this ceremony, other katsinas may appear at any time during the next six months.

POPULATION FIGURES
.... (1 January 1970)

PUEBLO INDIANS
(35,351)

TANOAN (10,017)

Tewa	3,658
Nambé	328
Pojoaque	107
San Ildefonso	358
San Juan	1,487
Santa Clara	1,119
Tesuque	259
Tiwa, northern	1,806
Picurís	163
Taos	1,623
Tiwa, southern	2,788
Isleta	2,527
Sandía	261
Guadalupe Indian Village	*
Towa	1,765
Jémez	1,765

KERESAN (13,675)

Keres, eastern	5,728
Cóchiti	779
San Felipe	1,632
Santa Ana	472
Santo Domingo	2,311
Zía	534

*Unknown

Keres, western	7,947
Acoma	2,861
Laguna	5,086

ZUÑIAN (5,640)

Zuñi	5,640

HOPI (6,019)

First Mesa	1,371
Polacca	755
Walpi	81
Sitchumovi	335
Hano (Tewa)	200
Second Mesa	1,435
Shipaulovi	202
Mishongnovi	426
Shungopavi	742
Sun Light Mission	65
Third Mesa	1,938
New Oraibi	720
Old Oraibi	180
Bacabi	238
Hotevila	800
Moencopi	1,019
Keams Canyon	256

THE ATHABASCANS
(ca. 140,100)

NAVAHO (126,267)

Chinle Agency	21,150
Eastern Navaho Agency	28,210
Cañoncito	ca. 1,125
Checkerboard	ca. 24,785
Puertocito (Alamo)	920
Ramah	1,380
Fort Defiance Agency	28,485
Shiprock Agency	25,379

Tuba City Agency	23,043

APACHE (13,837)

Jicarilla	1,742
Mescalero	ca. 1,740
Western Apache* (Ft. Apache, San Carlos)	ca. 10,355

*Arizona consus figures do not include off-reservation Indians.

THE UTE INDIANS (3,506)

UTE MOUNTAIN UTE

(Towaoc, Colo.)
(est. 1,146 enrolled)

SOUTHERN UTE

(Ignacio, Colo.) (760 enrolled)

NORTHERN UTE

(Ft. Duchesne, Utah) (1,600)

THE SOUTHERN PAIUTE (CA. 1,200)

KAIBAB PAIUTE

(over 100)

SHIVWITS PAIUTE

(150-200 enrolled)

CHEMEHUEVI

(now enrolled with Colo. River tribes) (ca. 600)

RANCHERIA PEOPLES (22,700)

COLORADO RIVER INDIAN TRIBES (4,451)

Chemehuevi, Mohave, Navaho, and Hopi together number 1,120 on reservation and 500 off reservation   *1,620*

Mohave at Fort Mohave (Parker, Ariz.)   *511*

Yuma (Quechan)—Ft. Yuma Reservation (1,007, plus 618 off reservation)   *1,625*

Cocopah (95 enrolled; includes ca. 300 in Mexico)   ca. 695

THE PAI (970)

Havasupai (eastern Pai)   ca. 270

Hualapai, or Walapai (western Pai)   ca. 685

Hualapai at Big Sandy, Ariz.   ca. 15

INDIANS OF THE SALT RIVER AGENCY (3,375)

Pima-Maricopa Community (1,700, plus 300 on nearby reservation)   2,000

Yavapai (Ft. McDowell Reservation)   ca. 300

Mohave-Apache (Ft. McDowell Reservation)   ca. 450

Yavapai Community   625
Yavapai-Apache (Camp Verde, Ariz.)   ca. 200

Tonto-Apache (Camp-Verde, Ariz.)   ca. 250

Yavapai at Prescott   ca. 90
"Payson Apache"   85

THE PIMANS (ca. 11,100)

Pima (river people)—Gila River Community; a few Maricopa and Papago included   enrolled: ca. 5,300

Papago (desert people)—main reservation   ca. 5,800

Maricopa—enumerated with Pima

THE CAHITANS (over 3,000)

Yaqui in Arizona   over 3,000

.........BIBLIOGRAPHY

Agogino, George A., and Michael L. Kunz (1971). "The Paleo Indian: Fact and Theory of Early Migrations to the New World," *The Indian Historian*, vol. 4, no. 1, Spring, pp. 21-26. The American Indian Historical Society. San Francisco.

Anderson, Jack (1969). "Papagos Living in Severe Poverty," Washington Merry-Go-Round, *Albuquerque Journal*, 15 November, pp. 3, 5.

_____ (1971). "Paiutes Nation's Most Deprived Tribe," *Albuquerque Journal*, 11 August.

Anonymous (1967). "Archeologists find Apache 'pueblos' near Las Vegas," *The New Mexican*, 23 April. Santa Fe.

_____ (1969a). "On Grand Canyon Floor. Havasupai Tribe to Get Houses," *Albuquerque Journal*, 15 June.

_____ (1969b). (On Navajo industries). *Arizona Republic*, 12 December. Phoenix.

_____ (1969c). "Indians: Squalor Amid Splendor," *Time*, 11 July. Chicago.

_____ (1969d). "White Mountain Apache Cattlemen," *New Mexico Stockman*, March, p. 49. Albuquerque.

_____ (1970a). "The Peyote Story," *Diné Baa Hane,* vol. 1, no. 11, August, pp. 12-13. Fort Defiance, Ariz.

_____ (1970b). "Ute Mountain Utes Ask Industrial Visits," *Albuquerque Journal*, 16 April.

_____ (1970c). "U.S. Government Honors Apache Tribes," *Albuquerque Journal*, 26 April: E-8.

_____ (1970d). "Indian Tribes Buy Part of Heritage," *The New Mexican*, 1 May. Santa Fe.

_____ (1970e). (On Hualapai Indians) *Albuquerque Journal*, 10 July.

_____ (1970f). "Zuni War Chief Dies," *The New Mexican*, 30 January. Santa Fe.

_____ (1970g). *Albuquerque Journal*, Action Line, 15 February.

_____ (1971a). "Arizona's 85 Payson Apaches Stump for Title to Tonto Land," *Albuquerque Journal*, 22 August: A-6 (Washington UPI)

_____ (1971b). "Luxury Complex Planned. Southern Ute Tribe Will Enter Tourist Business," *Albuquerque Journal*, 26 November.

_____(1971c). "Papago Indians Get Farm Grant," *Albuquerque Journal*, 25 December.

_____(1971d). "Indians Build $2 Million Resort," *The New Mexican*, 16 May. Santa Fe.

_____(1971e). "Master Potter of Maricopas Crushed to Death under Tree," *Arizona Republic*, 11 August, p. 21. Phoenix.

_____(1971f). "Ida Redbird Dies," *Newsletter*, The Heard Museum, September-October, Phoenix.

_____(1971g). "Fannin Asks Indian Aid," *The New Mexican*, 14 February. Santa Fe.

_____(1972). News Release, Window Rock, Ariz. 18 February.

_____(1973). *The New Mexican*, 5 August, p. B9. Santa Fe.

Arizona Commission of Indian Affairs (1971). *Tribal Directory.* 71 pp. Phoenix.

Arizona Writers' Project, WPA (1941). "The Apache," *Arizona Highways,* vol. xvii, no. 11, November, pp. 32-35, 42. Phoenix.

Bahti, Tom (1968). *Southwestern Indian Tribes.* KC Publications. Flagstaff.

Baldwin, Gordon C. (1965). *The Warrior Apaches.* Dale Stuart King. Tucson.

Ball, Eve (1970). *In The Days of Victorio.* Univ. of Arizona Press. Tucson.

Barnett, Franklin (1968). *Viola Jimulla: The Indian Chieftess.* Southwest Printers. Yuma, Ariz.

Bartel, Jon (1970). "First Indian High School Starts Classes at Ramah," *The Gallup Independent,* 12 August, p. 2B. Gallup, N. M.

Barton, Robert S. (1953). "The Lincoln Canes of the Pueblo Governors," *Lincoln Herald,* Winter, pp. 24-29.

Basehart, Harry W. (1967). "The Resource Holding Corp. Among the Mescalero Apache," *S. W. Journ. Anthro.*, vol. xxiii, pp. 277-291. Univ. of New Mexico Press. Albuquerque.

_____(1970). "Mescalero Apache Band Organization and Leadership," *S.W. Journ. Anthro.*, vol. xxvi, no. 1, pp. 87-104. Univ. of New Mexico Press. Albuquerque.

Berry, Norm (1971). "Light in the Desert," *Mountain Bell,* vol. ii, no. 2, Summer. Denver.

Bloom, Lansing B. (1940). "Who Discovered New Mexico?" *New Mexico Historical Review,* vol. xv, no. 2, April, pp. 101-132. Albuquerque.

Bolton, Herbert E. (1950). "Pageant in the Wilderness," *Utah Historical Quarterly*, vol. 18. Salt Lake City.

Brandon, William (1969). "American Indians: the Alien Americans," *The Progressive*, vol. xxxiii, no. 12, pp. 13-17. Madison, Wis.

_____(1970a). "The American Indians: the Un-Americans," *The Progressive*, January, pp. 35-39. Madison, Wis.

_____(1970b). "American Indians: the Real American Revolution," *The Progressive*, February, pp. 26-30. Madison, Wis.

Brennan, Bill (1966). "This is River Country," part one, The Colorado River Indian Reservation, pp. 9-11, 30-32; part two, Parker, Arizona—the Heart of the River Country, pp. 32-39 in *Arizona Highways*, vol. xlii, no. 2, February. Phoenix.

_____(1967). "Parker—Power Boat Racing Capital of the Southwest," *The Parker-Lake Havasu Story*, pp. 16-17. Phoenix.

Breuninger, Evelyn P. (1970). "Debut of Mescalero Maidens," *Apache Scout*, vol. xvi, no. 5, June, pp. 1-5. Mescalero Reservation. Mescalero, N. M.

Brugge, David M. (1969).   "A Navajo History," unpublished manuscript. 22 pp.

Bunzel, Ruth L. (1932a). "Introduction to Zuñi Ceremonialism," 47th Ann. Rep., *Bureau of American Ethnology*, pp. 471-544. Govt. Printing Office, Washington, D. C.

_____(1932b). Zuñi Katcinas: An Analytical Study," 47th Ann. Rep., *Bureau of American Ethnology*, pp. 843-903. Govt. Printing Office, Washington, D. C.

Carta Contenante le Royanne du Mexique et al Floride (n.d.) Old French map of early 1700s, in New Mexico State Record Center and Archives. Santa Fe.

Chaban, Ruth (1971). "The 1971 Annual Indian Market," *The Quarterly of the Southwestern Association on Indian Affairs, Inc.*, vol. vii, no. 2, Summer. Santa Fe.

Colton, Harold S. (1941). "Prehistoric Trade in the Southwest," *Scientific Monthly*, vol. 52, pp. 309-319. Amer. Assn. for the Advancement of Science. Washington, D. C.

Coues, Elliott (1900). *On the Trail of a Spanish Pioneer:* (the Diary and Itinerary of Francisco Garcés in his Travels Through Sonora, Arizona and California). 2 vols. Francis P. Harper. New York.

Coze, Paul (1952). "Of Clowns and Mudheads," *Arizona Highways*, vol. xxviii, no. 8, August, pp. 18-29. Phoenix.

_____(1971). "Living Spirits of Kachinam," *Arizona Highways,* Vol. xlvii, no. 6, June. Phoenix.

Cumming, Kendall (1967). Personal Letter, 21 April.

Davis, Irvine (1959). "Linguistic Clues to Northern Río Grande Prehistory," *El Palacio,* vol. 66, no. 3, June, pp. 73-83. Museum of N. M. Santa Fe.

Dittert, A.E., Jr. (1958). "Preliminary archaeological investigations in the Navajo project area of northwestern New Mexico,"

Papers in Anthro., no. 1, May, 25 pp., Museum of N. M. Press. Santa Fe.

_____(1959). "Culture Change in the Cebolleta Mesa Region, Central Western New Mexico," Doctoral dissertation, Univ. of Arizona (unpublished). Tucson.

_____(1967). Personal Information.

_____(1972). They came from the South," *Arizona Highways,* vol. xlviii, no. 1, January, pp. 34-39. Phoenix.

Dobyns, Henry F. and Robert C. Euler (1960). "A Brief History of the Northeastern Pai," *Plateau,* vol. 32, no. 3, January, pp. 49-56. Museum of No. Ariz. Flagstaff.

_____(1971). *The Havasupai People.* Indian Tribal Series. Phoenix.

Dobyns, Henry F., Paul H. Ezell, Alden W. Jones and Greta Ezell (1957). "Thematic Changes in Yuman Warfare: cultural stability and cultural change," *Proceedings,* Amer. Ethnol. Soc., pp. 46-71, annual spring meeting. Amer. Ethnol. Soc. Seattle.

Dockstader, Frederick J. (1954). *The Kachina and the White Man: A Study of the Influences of the White Culture on the Hopi Kachina Cult,* Bulletin no. 35. Cranbrook Institute of Science. Bloomfield Hills, Mich.

Douglas, F. H. (1931). "The Havasupai Indians," *Leaflet No. 33,* Denver Art Museum. 4 pp. Denver, Colo.

Drucker, Philip (1937). "Cultural Element Distributions:V" *Southern Calif. Anthropological Records,* vol. i, no. 1, Univ. of Calif. Press, Berkeley.

Dutton, Bertha P. (1963). *Sun Father's Way: The Kiva Murals of Kuana.* Univ. of N. M. Press. Albuquerque.

_____(1966). "Pots Pose Problems," *El Palacio,* vol. 73, no. 1, Spring, pp. 5-15. Museum of N. M. Press. Santa Fe.

_____(1972a) "The New Year of the Pueblo Indians of New Mexico," *El Palacio,* vol. 78, no. 1. Museum of N. M. Press.

_____(1972b). *Let's Explore: Indian Villages Past and Present.* Museum of N. M. press. 65 pp. Santa Fe.

Eddy, Frank W. (1965). "The Desert Culture of the Southwestern United States," Lecture at St. Michael's College (College of Santa Fe), 9 February (unpublished). Santa Fe.

_____(1966). "Prehistory in the Navajo Reservoir District, Northwestern New Mexico," *Papers in Anthro.*, no. 15, pt. I. Museum of N. M. Press. Santa Fe.

_____(1974). "Population dislocation in the Navaho reservoir district, New Mexico and Colorado," *Amer. Antiquity*, vol. 39, no. 1:75-84.

Eggan, Fred (1950). *Social Organization of the Western Pueblos.* Univ. of Chicago Press. Chicago.

Eklund, D. E. (1969). "Pendleton Blankets," *Arizona Highways*, vol. xlv, no. 8, August, p. 40. Phoenix.

Ellis, Florence (Hawley) (1964). "Archaeological History of Nambé Pueblo, 14th Century to Present," *American Antiquity*, vol. 30, no. 1, July, pp. 34-42. Soc. for Amer. Archaeology. Salt Lake City.

Emmitt, Robert (1954). *The Last War Trail – The Utes and the Settlement of Colorado.* Univ. of Oklahoma Press. Norman.

Euler, Robert C. (1961). "Aspects of Political Organization Among the Puertocito Navajo," *El Palacio*, vol. 68, no. 2, Summer, pp. 118-120. Museum of N.M. Santa Fe.

_____(1966). "Southern Paiute Ethnohistory," *Anthro. Papers.* no. 78, April. Univ. of Utah Press. Salt Lake City.

_____(1972a). *The Paiute People.* Indian Tribal Series. Phoenix.

_____(1972b). Personal Letter, 7 July.

Ezell, Greta S. and Paul H. Ezell (1970). "Background to Battle: Circumstances Relating to Death on the Gila, 1857," in *Troopers West: Military and Indian Affairs on the American Frontier*, pp. 169-186. Frontier Heritage Press. San Diego.

Faris, Chester E. (n.d.). "Pueblo Governors' Canes," Mimeographed report. 7 pp.

Fontana, B. L. (1967). Personal Letter, 6 January.

Fontana, B. L., Wm. J. Robinson, C. W. Cormack and E. E. Leavitt, Jr. (1962). *Papago Indian Pottery.* Univ. of Wash. Press. Seattle.

Forrest, Earle R. (1961). *The Snake Dance of the Hopi Indians.* Westernlore Press. Los Angeles.

Forrestal, Peter P. (transl.) and Cyprian J. Lynch (historical intro. and notes) (1954). *Benavides' Memorial of 1630.* Academy of Amer. Franciscan Hist. Washington, D. C.

Fort Mohave Tribal Council (California-Arizona-Nevada) (1970). *Letter and Resolution,* 27 October, 6 pp. Needles, Calif.

Fowler, Catherine S. (1971). Personal Letter, 14 June.

Fowler, Don D. and Catherine S. Fowler (Eds.) (1971). "Anthropology of the Numa: John Wesley Powell's manuscripts on the Numic Peoples of Western North America, 1868-1880," *Smithsonian Contributions to Anthro.,* No. 14, Smithsonian Institution. Washington, D. C.

Gabel, Norman E. (1949). *A Comparative Racial Study of the Papago,* Univ. of New Mexico Publications in Anthro., no. 4, Univ. of N. M. Press. Albuquerque.

Galvin, John (Transl. and Ed.) (1967). *A Record of Travels in Arizona and California, 1775-1776, Father Francisco Garcés.* John Howell Books. San Francisco.

Gerald, Rex E. (1958) "Two Wickiups on the San Carlos Indian Reservation, Arizona," *The Kiva,* vol. 23, no. 3, February, pp. 5-11. Ariz. Arch. and Hist. Society. Tucson.

Gilliland, H. M. (1972). Personal Letter and data sheets. *Hopi Indian Agency,* 16 March. Keams Canyon, Ariz.

Gonzales, Clara (1969). *The Shalakos Are Coming.* Museum of N. M. Press. 13 pp. Santa Fe.

Goodwin, Grenville (1942). *The Social Organization of the Western Apache.* Univ. of Chicago Press. Chicago.

Graves, Howard (1970). "Jobs, Tradition, Urbanization Key Navajo Race Factors," *Albuquerque Journal,* 24 August.

Gunnerson, James H. (1960). "An Introduction to Plains Apache Archaeology—the Dismal River Aspect," *B. A. E. Anthro. Paper No. 58.* Washington, D. C.

_____(1969a). "Apache Archaeology in Northeastern New Mexico," *American Antiquity,* vol. 34, pp. 23-39. Soc. for Amer. Archaeology. Salt Lake City.

_____(1969b). "Archaeological Survey on and near Pecos National Monument—Preliminary Report," mimeographed report, pp. 1-9.

Gunnerson, James H. and Dolores A. (1970). "Evidence of Apaches at Pecos," *El Palacio,* vol. 76, no. 3, pp. 1-6, Museum of N. M. Santa Fe.

_____(1971a). "Apachean Culture: A Study in Unity and Diversity," reprinted from *Apachean Culture History and Ethnology, Anthro. Papers, No. 21,* pp. 7-22. Univ. of Ariz, Tucson.

_____(1971b). "Apachean Culture History and Ethnology," *Anthro. Papers, No. 21,* 22 pp., Univ. of Ariz. Tucson.

Hackett, Charles Wilson (1937). *Historical Documents Relating to*

New Mexico, Nueva Vizcaya, and Approaches thereto, to 1773. 3 vols. Carnegie Institution. Washington, D. C.

Hanlon, C. J. (O. F. M.) (1972). "Papago Funeral Customs," *The Kiva,* vol. 37, no. 2, Winter, pp. 104-112. Ariz. Arch. and Hist. Society. Tucson.

Harrington, John P. (1940). "Southern Peripheral Athapaskawàn Origins, Divisions, and Migrations," *Essays in Historical Anthropology of North America, Smithsonian Misc. Colls.,* vol. 100, pp. 503-532. Smithsonian Institution, Washington, D. C.

Hawley, Florence (1950). "Big Kivas, Little Kivas, and Moiety Houses in Historical Reconstruction," *S. W. Journal of Anthro.,* vol. 6, no. 3, Autumn, pp. 286-300. Univ. of N. M. Press. Albuquerque.

Hawley, Florence and Donovan Senter (1946). "Group-designed Behavior Patterns in Two Acculturating Groups," *S. W. Journal of Anthro.,* vol. 2, no. 2, pp. 133-151. Univ. of N. M. Press. Albuquerque.

Hayes, George (1971). Personal Information. Pojoaque, New Mexico, 18 November.

Hester, James J. (1962). "Early Navajo Migrations and Acculturation in the Southwest," *Papers in Anthro.* no. 6, 131 pp. Museum of N. M. Press. Santa Fe.

Hewett, E. L. and B. P. Dutton (1945). *The Pueblo Indian World.* Univ. of N. M. Press. Albuquerque.

Hill, W. W. (1940). "Some Aspects of Navajo Political Structure," *Plateau,* vol. 13, no. 2. Reprint, 6 pp. Museum of No. Ariz. Flagstaff.

Hodge, Frederick W. (Ed.) (1910). "Handbook of American Indians North of Mexico," *B. A. E. Bull. 30,* part two: p. 186. Smithsonian Institution. Washington, D. C.

Hoebel, E. Adamson (1958). *Man in the Primitive World.* McGraw-Hill Book Co. New York, London and Toronto.

Hoijer, Harry (1938). *Chiricahua and Mescalero Apache Texts.* Univ. of Chicago Press. Chicago.

_____(1956) "The Chronology of the Athapaskan Languages," *International Journal of American Linguistics,* vol. 22, no. 4, October, pp. 219-232. Baltimore.

Hoijer, Harry et al. (1963). "Studies in the Athapaskan Languages," *Publications in Linguistics,* University of California.

Hopi Reservation. (a mimeographed leaflet of information) issued by the Hopi Tribe. 13 pp. Keams Canyon, Ariz.

Houser, Nicholas P. (1972). "The Camp"—An Apache Community of Payson, Arizona," *The Kiva*, vol. 37, no. 2, Winter, pp. 65-71. Ariz. Arch. and Hist. Society. Tucson.

Hume, Bill (1970a). "Sandia Pueblo Adopts Best of Two Cultures," *Albuquerque Journal*, 9 August, p. D-1.

_____(1970b). "Prehistoric Site, Scenic Canyon Boost Santa Clara's Finances," *Albuquerque Journal*, 4 October, p. G-1.

_____(1974). "The Havasupai Prisoners of Grand Canyon," *Indian Affairs*, No. 86 (Newsletter). March-April, pp. 1-2, 7. New York.

Huscher, B. H. and H. A. (1942). "Athapascan Migration via the Intermontane Region," *American Antiquity*, vol. 8, no. 1, pp. 80-88. Soc. for Amer. Archaeology. Menasha, Wis.

_____(1943). "The Hogan Builders of Colorado," *Colorado Archaeological Society*. Gunnison, Colo.

James, Harry C. (1956). *The Hopi Indians*. The Caxton Press. Caldwell, Idaho.

Johnston, Bernice (1970). *Speaking of Indians*. Univ. of Arizona Press. Tucson.

Kaut, Charles R. (1957). "The Western Apache Clan System: Its Origins and Development," *Publications in Anthro.*, no. 9, 85 pp. Univ. of New Mexico. Albuquerque.

Kelly, Dorothea S. (1950). "A Brief History of the Cocopa Indians of the Colorado River Delta," in *For the Dean*, pp. 159-169. Hohokam Museums Association and the Southwestern Monuments Association. Tucson, Arizona and Santa Fe, N. M.

Kelly, Isabel (1964). "Southern Paiute Ethnography," *Anthro. Papers*, No. 69. May. Univ. of Utah Press. Salt Lake City.

Kelly, William H. (1953). *Indians of the Southwest: A Survey of Indian Tribes and Indian Administration in Arizona*. 1st Ann. Rep. Bureau of Ethnic Research, Dept. Anthro., 129 pp. Tucson.

King, William S. (1967). Information from Salt River Indian Agency, Scottsdale, Arizona, 11 April, 3 pp.

Kluckhohn, Clyde and Dorothea Leighton (1962). *The Navajo*. Doubleday & Co., Inc. Garden City, N. Y.

Kluckhohn, Clyde and Leland C. Wyman (1940). "An Introduction to Navaho Chant Practice," *Memoirs*, no. 53, Amer. Anthro. Assn. Menasha, Wis.

Kurath, William and Edward H. Spicer (1947). "A Brief Introduction to Yaqui, a Native Language of Sonora," *Bulletin* (Social Science Bull. no. 15) Univ. of Ariz. Tucson.

Levy, Jerrold E. (1965). "Navajo Suicide," *Human Organization,* vol. 24. no. 4, pp. 308-318. Soc. for Applied Anthro. Ithaca, N. Y.

Levy, Jerrold E., Stephen J. Kunitz, and Michael Everett (1969). "Navajo Criminal Homicide," *S.W. Jrnl. of Anthro.*, vol. 25, no. 2, Summer, pp. 124-149. Univ. of N. M. Albuquerque.

Link, Martin A. (1968). (Introduction to) *Treaty between the United States of America and the Navajo Tribe of Indians*, KC Publications. Flagstaff, Ariz.

Lister, Robert H. (1958). "Archaeological Excavations in the Northern Sierra Madre Occidental, Chihuahua and Sonora, Mexico," *Univ. of Colorado Studies*, Series in Anthropology, no. 7. Boulder.

Lumholtz, Carl (1902). *Unknown Mexico*, 2 vols. Charles Scribner's Sons. New York.

McGregor, John C. (1951). *The Cohonina Culture of Northwestern Arizona*. Univ. of Illinois Press. Urbana, Illinois.

_____(1967). *The Cohonina Culture of Mount Floyd, Arizona*. Univ. of Kentucky Press. Lexington, Ky.

McNitt, Frank (1970). "Fort Sumner: a Study in Origins," *New Mexico Historical Review*, April, pp. 101-115. Albuquerque.

Mangel, Charles (1970). "Sometimes We Feel We're Already Dead," *Look*, vol. 34, no. 11, 2 June, pp. 38-43. New York.

Martin, John (1972). Personal Letter. 3 April.

Matthews, Washington (1887). "The Mountain Chant: A Navajo Ceremony," Bureau American Ethnology, pp. 385-467. Washington, D. C.

_____(1897). *Navaho Legends*. American Folklore Society. New York.

_____(1902) "The Night Chant, a Navaho Ceremony," *Memoirs*, vol. vi, May. American Museum of Nat. Hist. New York.

Miller, Wick R. and C. G. Booth (1972). "The Place of Shoshoni among American Languages," *Introduction to Shoshoni Language Course Materials*. Aug. 9 pp. Owyhee, Nevada.

Montgomery, Ross Gordon, Watson Smith and J. O. Brew (1949). "Franciscan Awatovi, the Excavation and Conjectural Reconstruction of a 17th Century Spanish Mission Establishment at a Hopi Indian Town in Northeastern Arizona," *Papers, Peabody Mus. of Amer. Arch. and Ethnol.*, vol. xxxvi. Harvard Univ., Cambridge.

Montgomery, William (1970a). "Fruitland Mine, Plant Liked," *Albuquerque Journal*, 18 August, pp. A-1 and A-5.

_____(1970b). "Black Mesa Coal Provides Indians Jobs," *Albu-*

querque *Journal*, 19 August, pp. A-1 and A-5.

_____(1970c). "Navajo Generating Plant Now Building," *Albu-querque Journal,* 22 August, pp. A-1 and A-5.

_____(1970d). "Water Key to Southwest's Growth," *Albuquerque Journal,* 26 August, pp. A-1 and A-5.

Morris, Clyde P. (1972). "Yavapai-Apache Family Organization in a Reservation Context," *Plateau,* vol. 44, no. 3, Winter, pp. 105-110. Museum of No. Ariz. Flagstaff.

Murray, Clyde A. (1969). "Homes in Flood Plain: CAP to Displace Indians," *The Arizona Republic,* 9 November, p. 24-B. Phoenix.

Moon, Sheila (1970). *A Magic Dwells.* Wesleyan Univ. Press. Middletown, Conn.

Nabokov, Peter (1969). "The Peyote Road," *The New York Times Magazine,* Sec. 6, 9 March, pp. 30-31, 129-132, 134.

Navajo Census Office (1970). Window Rock, Arizona.

Navajo Community College (n.d.). *Introducing the Navajo Community College,* 25 pp. brochure.

Navajo Tribal Museum (1968). *Historical Calendar of the Navajo People.* 15 July. Window Rock, Arizona.

New, Lloyd (1968). "Institute of American Indian Arts, Cultural Difference as the Basis for Creative Education," *Native American Arts,* no. 1. U. S. Dept. of the Interior, San Francisco. Washington, D. C.

Opler, Morris E. (1935). "The Concept of Supernatural Power Among the Chiricahua and Mescalero Apaches," *American Anthro.,* vol. 37, pp. 65-70. Menasha, Wis.

_____(1938a). Ethnological Notes in *Chiricahua and Mescalero Apache Texts,* by Harry Hoijer. Univ. of Chicago Press. Chicago.

_____(1938b). "Myths and Tales of the Jicarilla Apache Indians," *Memoirs* of the Amer. Folklore Society, vol. 31, 393 pp. New York.

_____(1941). *An Apache Life-Way; The Economic, Social, and Religious Institutions of the Chiricahua Indians.* Univ. of Chicago Press. Chicago.

_____(1942). "Myths and Tales of the Chiricahua Apache Indians," *Memoirs* of the Amer. Folklore Society, vol. xxxvii, 101 pp. New York.

_____(1943). "Navaho Shamanistic Practice Among the Jicarilla Apache," *New Mexico Anthropologist,* vols. vi, vii, no. 1. Jan.-Mar., pp. 13-18. Univ. of Chicago Press.

Ortiz, Alfonso (1969). *The Tewa World.* Univ. of Chicago Press. Chicago and London.

Painter, Muriel Thayer and E. B. Sayles (1962). *Faith, Flowers and Fiestas.* Univ. of Arizona Press. Tucson.

Papago Indian Agency (1970). *Facts about the Papago Indian Reservation and the Papago People.* (Mimeographed.) 12 pp. Sells, Ariz.

Parsons, Elsie Clews (1925). *The Pueblo of Jemez.* Phillips Academy. Andover, Mass.

_____(1939). *Pueblo Indian Religion.* 2 vols. Univ. of Chicago Press. Chicago.

Powell, John W. (1891). "Indian Linguistic Families of America North of Mexico." Bureau American Ethnology, *7th Ann. Rep.* Washington, D. C.

Reed, Verner Z. (1896). "The Ute Bear Dance," *American Anthro.,* vol. ix, July, pp. 237-244. Menasha, Wis.

Reichard, Gladys A. (1963). *Navaho Religion,* Bollingen Series 18, Pantheon Books. New York

Richards, David (1970). "America's Silent Minority," *TWA Ambassador,* vol. 3, no. 5, pp. 7-12. St. Paul, Minn.

Robinson, A. E. (Bert) (1954). *The Basket Weavers of Arizona.* Univ. of N.M. Press. Albuquerque.

Sandoval, H. (1971). "Views on 'A Gunfight,' " *The Jicarilla Chieftain,* 1 November. Dulce, New Mexico. (editorial)

Sapir, Edward (1929). "Central and North American Languages," in *The Encyclopaedia Britannica* (14th Ed.), vol. 5, pp. 139-141.

Schaafsma, Polly (1966). *Early Navaho Rock Paintings and Carvings.* Museum of Navaho Ceremonial Art, Inc. Santa Fe.

Schevill, Margaret Erwin (1947). *Beautiful on the Earth.* Hazel Dreis Editions. Santa Fe.

Schoenwetter, James and A. E. Dittert, Jr. (1968). "An Ecological Interpretation of Anasazi Settlement Patterns," in *Anthropological Archaeology in the Americas.* The Anthro. Society of Washington. pp. 41-61. Washington, D. C.

Schroeder, Albert H. (1963). "Navajo and Apache Relationships West of the Rio Grande," *El Palacio,* vol. 70, no. 3, Autumn, pp. 5-20. Museum of New Mexico. Santa Fe.

Schwartz, Douglas W. (1956). "The Havasupai 600 A.D.—1955 A.D.: A Short Culture History," *Plateau,* vol. 28, no. 4, April, pp. 77-84. Museum of No. Ariz. Flagstaff.

_____(1959). "Culture Area and Time Depth: the Four Worlds of the Havasupai," *American Anthro.*, vol. 61, no. 6, December, pp. 1060-1069. Menasha, Wis.

Shepardson, Mary (1963). "Navajo Ways in Government (a Study in Political Process)," *Memoir 96*, Amer. Anthro. Assn. vol. 65, no. 3, pt. 2, June. Menasha, Wis.

Smith, Anne (1965). *New Mexico Indians Today*. A report prepared as part of the N. M. State Resources Development Plan. Museum of N. M. June, 279 pp. Santa Fe.

_____(1966). *New Mexico Indians:* Economic, educational, and social problems. Museum of N. M., Research Records no. 1. 58 pp. Santa Fe.

_____(1968). *Indian Education in New Mexico.* Div. of Govt. Research, Institute for Social Research and Dev. Univ. of N. M., July, 49 pp. Albuquerque.

_____(1974). *Ethnography of the Northern Ute.* Museum of N. M. Press. Papers in Anthropology no. 17. 285 pp. Santa Fe.

Smith, Watson (1952). "Kiva Mural Decorations at Awatovi and Kawaika-a, with a Survey of Other Wall Paintings in the Pueblo Southwest," *Papers*, Peabody Mus. of Amer. Arch. and Ethnol., Harvard Univ., vol. xxxvii. Reports of the Awatovi Exped. Report no. 5. Cambridge.

_____(1971). "Painted Ceramics of the Western Mound at Awatovi," *Papers*, Peabody Mus. of Amer. Arch. and Ethnol., Harvard Univ., no. 38. Cambridge.

Sonnichsen, C. L. (1958). *The Mescalero Apaches.* Univ. of Oklahoma Press. Norman, Okla.

Southwestern Monuments Monthly Report, Supplement for November (1937). U. S. Dept. of Interior, Natl. Park Service. p. 396. Coolidge, Ariz.

Spencer, Katherine (1947). *Reflection of Social Life in the Navaho Origin Myth.* Univ. of N. M. Press. Albuquerque.

Spencer, Robert (1940). "A Preliminary Sketch of Keresan Grammar," Master's Thesis, Univ. of New Mexico (unpublished).

Spicer, Edward H. (1970). *Cycles of Conquest* (the impact of Spain, Mexico, and the United States on the Indians of the Southwest 1533-1960). Univ. of Ariz. Press. Tucson.

Spicer, Edward H., Phyllis Balastrero, and Ted DeGrazia (1971). "Yaqui Easter Ceremonial," *Arizona Highways,* vol. xlvii, no. 3, March, pp. 2-10, 11, 34, 45-47. Phoenix.

Spier, Leslie (1928). "Havasupai Ethnography," *Anthro. Papers,* Amer. Museum of Natural History, vol. 29, pt. 3:286. New York.

_____(1955). "Mohave Culture Items," *Bulletin 28*, Museum of Northern Arizona, Northern Arizona Society of Science and Art, Inc. Flagstaff.

Spinden, Herbert J. (Transl.)(1933). *Songs of the Tewa.* New York.

Stephen, Alexander M. (E. C. Parsons, Ed.) (1936). *Hopi Journal*, 2 vols., Columbia Univ. Contribs. to Anthro., vol. 23. New York.

Steward, Julian H. (1955). *Theory of Culture Change.* Univ. of Illinois Press. Urbana, Illinois.

Stewart, Kenneth M. (1967). "Chemehuevi Culture Changes." *Plateau,* vol. 40, no. 1, Summer, pp. 14-20. Museum of Northern Arizona. Flagstaff.

Strong, William Duncan (1927). "An Analysis of Southwestern Society," *American Anthropologist,* vol. 29, no. 1, Jan.-Mar. 1927. Menasha, Wis.

Swadish, Morris (1967). "Linguistic Classification in the Southwest," in *Studies in Southwestern Ethnolinguistics,* pp. 281-306. Mouton & Co. The Hague and Paris.

Swanton, John R. (1952) "The Indian Tribes of North America," Bur. of Amer. Ethnology, Smithsonian Inst., *Bull. 145.* Washington, D.C.

Taylor, Morris F. (1970). "Campaigns Against the Jicarilla Apache, 1855," *New Mexico Historical Review,* April, pp. 119-133. Albuquerque.

Thrapp, Dan L. (1967). "Christian Missions Bested: 45% of Navajos Accept Peyote-Oriented Church," *Los Angeles Times,* 17 August.

Trager, George L. (1969). "Navajo Mountain—Navaho Molehill?" *Newsletter*, Amer. Anthro. Assn., p. 2. Menasha, Wis.

Uintah and Ouray Agency (Ute) (1970). Letter, 3 September. Fort Duchesne, Utah.

Underhill, Ruth M. (1938a). "A Papago Calender Record," *Bull., Anthro. Series,* vol. 2, no. 5, 1 March, 64 pp. Albuquerque.

_____(1938b). *Singing for Power.* Univ. of Calif. Press. Berkeley.

_____(1940). *The Papago Indians of Arizona,* Sherman Pamphlets, no. 3, 63 pp. Education Division, U. S. Office of Indian Affairs.

Ute Mountain Ute Agency, Towaoc, Colorado (n.d.[a], 1969?). "The American Indians of Colorado," 5 pp. Mimeographed report.

_____(n.d.[b], 1969?). "A Brief History of the Colorado Utes," 3 pp. Mimeographed report.

_____(1970). Letter, 18 August.

Van Valkenburgh, Richard (1945). "The Government of the Navajos," *Ariz. Quarterly,* vol. 1, pp. 63-73. Univ. of Ariz. Press. Tucson.

Vestal, Paul A. (1952). "Ethnobotany of the Rimrock Navaho," *Papers.* Peabody Mus. of Amer. Arch. and Ethnol., vol. 40, no. 4. Harvard Univ. Cambridge.

Vogt, Evon Z. (1951). "Navaho Veterans—a Study of Changing Values," *Papers,* Peabody Mus. of Amer. Arch. and Ethnol., vol. xli, no. 1. Harvard Univ. Cambridge.

Waliczed, John (1970). "Navajo High School Opens Door at Home," *The New Mexican,* 6 September (from Gallup Independent for AP). Santa Fe.

Walker, George W. (1970). "Celebrating the Arrival of Dr. Charles H. Cook, after Whom Cook Training School is Named, at Sacaton, Arizona," *Indian Highways*, no. 134, December, pp. 4 and 6. Cook Christian Training School. Tempe, Ariz.

White, Leslie A. (1935). "The Pueblo of Santo Domingo, New Mexico," *Memoirs* of the Amer. Anthro. Assn., no. 43, pp. 1-210. Menasha, Wis.

Whitfield, Charles (1971). Personal Information, long distance phone call, 11 May.

Whiting, Alfred F. (1958). "Havasupai Characteristics in the Cohonina," *Plateau*, vol. 30, no. 30, January, pp. 55-60. Museum of No. Ariz. Flagstaff.

Whitman, William III (1947). "The Pueblo Indians of San Ildefonso," *Contribs. to Anthropology, Columbia Univ.* no. 34. New York.

Willey, Gordon R. (1966). *An Introduction to American Archaeology*, vol. I. Prentice-Hall, Inc. Englewood Cliffs, New Jersey.

Yazzie, Ethelou (Ed.) (1971). *Navajo History,* vol. I. Navajo Community College Press. Many Farms, Arizona.

Young, Robert W. (1961). "The Origin and Development of Navajo Tribal Government," *The Navajo Yearbook,* Report no. viii, 1951-1961 a Decade of Progress, pp. 371-392. Navajo Agency. Window Rock, Ariz.

_____(1968). *The Role of the Navajo in the Southwestern Drama.* Robert W. Young and *The Gallup Independent.* Galley, N.M.

Young, Robert W., and William Morgan (1943). *The Navaho Language.* Education Div., U. S. Indian Service Phoenix.